Lift Up Your Heads, O Ye Gates

Dr. Royce L Woods

TRILOGY CHRISTIAN PUBLISHERS

TUSTIN, CA

Trilogy Christian Publishers
A Wholly Owned Subsidiary of Trinity Broadcasting Network
2442 Michelle Drive
Tustin, CA 92780

Lift Up Your Heads, O Ye Gates

Trilogy Christian Publishers,
A Wholly Owned Subsidiary of Trinity Broadcasting Network
2442 Michelle Drive Tustin, CA 92780

Unless otherwise indicated, Scripture quotations marked KJV are taken from the King James Version of the Bible. Public domain.

Scripture quotations marked MSG are taken from THE MESSAGE, copyright © 1993, 2002, 2018 by Eugene H. Peterson. Used by permission of NavPress. All rights reserved. Represented by Tyndale House Publishers, Inc.

Rights Department, 2442 Michelle Drive, Tustin, CA 92780.

Trilogy Christian Publishing/TBN and colophon are trademarks of Trinity Broadcasting Network.

Cover design by Jeff Summers

For information about special discounts for bulk purchases, please contact Trilogy Christian Publishing.

Trilogy Disclaimer: The views and content expressed in this book are those of the author and may not necessarily reflect the views and doctrine of Trilogy Christian Publishing or the Trinity Broadcasting Network.

Manufactured in the United States of America

10 9 8 7 6 5 4 3 2 1

Library of Congress Cataloging-in-Publication Data is available.

ISBN: 978-1-68556-420-9

E-ISBN: 978-1-68556-421-6

And the LORD answered me, and said, Write the vision, and make it plain upon tables, that he may run that readeth it. For the vision is yet for an appointed time, but at the end it shall speak, and not lie: though it tarry, wait for it; because it will surely come, it will not tarry.

—Habakkuk 2:2–3

Dedication

This work is dedicated to all the faithful servants of Christ, many worshiping together in what are being called underground churches, who, despite living under constant threats of physical harm or worse, continue to embrace that which God has sown into their hearts. May their trumpets be sounded from one end of the earth to the other, as their unwavering commitments truly deserve the highest degree of honor and reverence.

Acknowledgements

To my loving parents, John and Mary Woods, whose contribution to this work goes without saying. The unselfish love they shared with us during our formative years is unsurpassed by any challenge I have ever encountered in my life.

All glory, honor, and praise belong to the one true and living God, who is the Creator of both heaven and earth.
Through Him and Him alone, have we received two *infallible gifts*:
an *idea* and a *solution*...
The idea is *love*. The solution is *blood*.
Without love, there is only sorrow, sickness, suffering, and pain. And without *blood*...there is no life, only death.
With His love, God has validated us, and with His *blood*, He has...
vindicated us.

—Dr. R. L. Woods

God is up to something new. It's bigger than Messianic Judaism. It's bigger than Gentile Christianity. Both have been used mightily by God, but this new move will not look like a traditional synagogue, a traditional church, or even a Messianic synagogue, although it will have aspects of each. It will not be the one-man show, but the one new man. It is Jewish and Gentile believers holding the baton together. The two have been made one in Jesus.

—Sid Roth
The Race to Save the World

So we are in a time of mutual awakening and a time of mutual activation. It is a time to make a stand and a time to move out and win new territory.

Tasks lie before us. Whether we are Jewish or Gentile, it is time to pray and proclaim, to give and receive. For some of us, it is time to take radical action.

God promises help, prosperity, and provision to those who formally set themselves against His name and His people. Of course, for everyone, a choice is involved. Everybody can choose to accept the offer or not. Those who accept will have a front-row seat as the final drama unfolds.

—James W. Goll
The Coming Israel Awakening

Looking for that blessed hope, and the glorious appearing of the great God and our Saviour Jesus Christ.

—Titus 2:13

Contents

Preface

Unto the angel of the church of Ephesus write; These things saith he that holdeth the seven stars in his right hand, who walketh in the midst of the seven golden candlesticks; I know thy works, and thy labour, and thy patience, and how thou canst not bear them which are evil: and thou hast tried them which say they are apostles, and are not, and hast found them liars: And hast borne, and hast patience, and for my name's sake hast laboured, and hast not fainted. Nevertheless I have somewhat against thee, because thou hast left thy first love. Remember therefore from whence thou art fallen, and repent, and do the first works; or else I will come unto thee quickly, and will remove thy candlestick out of his place, except thou repent. But this thou hast, that thou hatest the deeds of the Nicolaitanes, which I also hate. He that hath an ear, let him hear what the Spirit saith unto the churches; To him that over-

*cometh will I give to eat of the tree of life, which is in
the midst of the paradise of God.*

—Revelation 2:1–7

Imagine living in a world where miracles and multiplied blessings are commonplace, where the kind of optimism that love and caring produce become the order of the day. This is the promised fruit of the candlestick (the Church, Revelation 1:20), which houses the anointed Word of God, being augmented or strengthened by the angel assigned to it. The advice in this letter is prophetic, forewarning present-day Christians of the snares that can lure us away from the faith. For this reason, without the presence of the candlestick—*God's Renascent Church*—the dynamics that are currently at play in the earth, such as global warming, unchecked viruses, financial collapse, moral decay, and man's continued inhumanity against his fellow man, will continue to go unabated and unchallenged. Today more than ever, there are so many people who are aimlessly and blindly walking around, totally devoid of divine direction; all their true purpose has been shrouded in darkness—mentally, emotionally, and most of all, spiritually.

That's why there must be a profound word, one that can act as a beacon, a word foretold by God that offers foresight and allows navigation around those obstacles that normally would not be seen.

Thy word is a lamp unto my feet, and a light unto my path.

—Psalm 119:105

Both the apostles Paul and Peter take us more in depth as we explore this remarkable anomaly.

But he that prophesieth speaketh unto men to edification, and exhortation, and comfort.

—1 Corinthians 14:3

And it shall come to pass in the last days, saith God, I will pour out of my Spirit upon all flesh: and your sons and your daughters shall prophesy, and your young men shall see visions, and your old men shall dream dreams: And on my servants and on my handmaidens I will pour out in those days of my Spirit; and they shall prophesy.

—Acts 2:17–18

The apostle Peter, in quoting the prophet Joel, clearly spells out the season and time in which we are currently living, *"the last days"*; this verse and others like it have reaffirmed our Great Commission to prepare the way for the imminent return of the great I AM.

Verily, verily, I say unto you, He that believeth on me, the works that I do shall he do also; and greater works than these shall he do; because I go unto my Father.

—John 14:12

However, there are other crucial components to this montage of believers that God has assembled for His purpose.

And he gave some, apostles; and some, prophets; and some, evangelists; and some, pastors and teachers.
—Ephesians 4:11

This book was written purely from a prophetic perspective, as our emphasis here is to further advance this amazing historical idea (love) and to better analyze this God-given solution (blood). As dreamers and visionaries, we also seek counsel from a Higher Power, One whom we believe has the profound ability to create, plan, direct, and alter global events. However, for His plan to manifest itself, we must first be willing to return to Him that which He has created for His own purpose—or, as the Bible puts it, "His good pleasure."

Fear not, little flock; for it is your Father's good pleasure to give you the kingdom.
—Luke 12:32

This Kingdom that Jesus was referring to extends from everlasting to everlasting, although throughout time, only a select few understood the direct correlation between their very existence and future events. What an honor it must have been to recognize with a heightened sense of awareness, not only who they were, but also their relationship to God's *grand scheme* of things.

> *Open to me the gates of righteousness: I will go into them, and I will praise the LORD: This gate of the LORD, into which the righteous shall enter. I will praise thee: for thou hast heard me, and art become my salvation. The stone which the builders refused is become the head stone of the corner. This is the LORD's doing; it is marvellous in our eyes.*
>
> —Psalm 118:19–23

This Messianic psalm is all the verification needed to confirm that the dreams and prophetic visions those elders received were designed to spiritually carry them along an astonishing road, one that was fully intended to expose them to places and events that had yet to be seen or experienced. And just as with the psalmist in our text, all along this proverbial road, while being used to launch and sustain the Church's history, there have been many Hebrew and Jewish gates (patriarchs) whom God would use to open doors for others ("...*Joshua said to the people, Shout; for the LORD hath given you the city"* [Joshua 6:16]), but only one *Gatekeeper*, whose blood-washed port of entry would be opened to all, *Jesus Christ our Lord.*

> *I am the door: by me if any man enter in, he shall be saved, and shall go in and out, and find pasture.*
> —John 10:9

> *Wherefore also we pray always for you, that our God would count you worthy of this calling, and fulfil all the good pleasure of his goodness, and the work of faith with power.*
> —2 Thessalonians 1:11

This scripture clearly points out that there is power in our believing.

Introduction

Lift Up Your Heads, O Ye Gates highlights the four basic facets, or features, of the Christian experience.

When we think of these aspects, we don't use terms like "distinct" or "separate," because God's work is not only masterful but also seamless, which means that in the end, it all intertwines into one Lord, one faith, and one baptism.

1. From the very beginning, the Bible clearly shows that Jesus was not an afterthought, that from Genesis to the time of His birth, He was always at the forefront of God's magnificent plan, even to God's replacing Adam's fig leaves with animal skins, showing that in order for one to be truly covered in the eyes of God, there must first be a sacrificial offering, which included the spilling of blood.

2. The second facet tells us that the history of the Hebrew and Jewish people and the history of the Church are all one and the same. That's why in the book of Mat-

thew, the writer brings us down through those forty-two generations.

3. As all through those periods up to this present time, God's plan for the modern-day Church was always apparent, which is something that's been emphasized over and again by prophets such as Isaiah, Haggai, and Daniel, just to name a few.

> *For unto us a Child is born.*
>
> —Isaiah 9:6

> *The glory of this latter house shall be greater than of the former.*
>
> —Haggai 2:9

In the book of Daniel, the prophet speaks about earthly kings and their ultimate destruction, but in Daniel 2:44, he states, *"And in the days of these kings shall the God of heaven set up a kingdom, which shall never be destroyed."*

4. And this brings us to the fourth phase of the Christian experience. In it, God has been both persistent and adamant over the fact that during this time (the last days), there will be a shaking that none will be able to ignore. In Matthew 24:8, Jesus calls it *"the beginning of sorrows,"* but He also says, *"See that ye be not troubled...the end is not yet"* (verse 6). Why? The Scriptures tell us.

And it shall come to pass in the last days, saith God, I will pour out of my Spirit upon all flesh: and your sons and your daughters shall prophecy, your young men shall see visions, and your old men shall dream dreams.

—Acts 2:17

Verily, verily, I say unto you, He that believeth on me, the works that I do shall he do also; and greater works than these shall he do; because I go unto my Father.

—John 14:12

All these facets are addressed in detail through this work, which is intended to advance the Body of Christ onward toward this well-timed, exhilarating clarion call. Though God has given us bite-sized pieces through the dispensational periods, it's all-inclusive of the main course.

And he said unto him, Oh my Lord, wherewith shall I save Israel? behold, my family is poor in Manasseh, and I am the least in my father's house.

—Judges 6:15

This statement was made almost three thousand years ago by an Old Testament figure who went by the name of Gideon. When Gideon was approached by the angel of God, the angel found him hiding in fear from Israel's enemies, the Midianites. However, Gideon was baffled by the angel's greeting.

> *"The LORD is with thee, thou mighty man of valour."*
>
> —Judges 6:12

Just as many who were called by God have done and still do, Gideon immediately proceeded to set the record straight. His response was, "There is no way you can be talking to me; 'my family is poor in Manasseh, and I am the least in my father's house.' In other words, I am just an ordinary man." But Gideon was soon to learn, just as I have learned, that God loves to use ordinary people to do extraordinary things.

> *I will praise thee; for I am fearfully and wonderfully made: marvellous are thy works; and that my soul knoweth right well.*
>
> —Psalm 139:14

After years of intense reflection, it has become increasingly clear to me that despite our human frailties, all who come this way, if only for a moment, have been given by our Creator a particular fragment or swatch of this huge puzzle of which only He (God) has the total picture. That's why it's not prudent or wise to argue with Him when He says this is how a certain thing must be done, all by following His direction, in order for His people to experience a greater degree of fulfillment and purpose in their lives. My purpose here with this treatment is to share revelation, a revealed knowledge. Therefore, it's not based on my opinion, but rather it's based solely on *God's positioning* and His place in our lives. The time for statements like "something told me" is over, as God is revealing Himself to those of His choosing with pinpoint accuracy.

> *And ye shall know the truth, and the truth shall make you free.*
>
> —John 8:32

The key is being watchful and perceptive to God's call.

> *Now Samuel did not yet know the LORD, neither was the word of the LORD yet revealed unto him. And the LORD called Samuel again the third time. And he arose and went to Eli, and said, Here am I;*

*for thou didst call me. And Eli perceived that the
LORD had called the child.*

—1 Samuel 3:7–8

Samuel didn't recognize the voice of God, but when
the time was right, God revealed Himself to the child
through Eli, the priest, and from that time on, Samuel
was off to the races.

*And Samuel grew, and the LORD was with him,
and did let none of his words fall to the ground.*

—1 Samuel 3:19

I get so excited when I think about how God is going to move on those who, like both Gideon and Samuel,
are currently unaware of the total plan for their lives;
that is, until *"the day dawn, and the day star arise in [their]
hearts"* (2 Peter 1:19).

*We then, as workers together with him, beseech you
also that ye receive not the grace of God in vain.*

—2 Corinthians 6:1

The word "grace" in this text can easily be interpreted
as "a gift." Since the power to perform lies squarely in
the hands of God, Paul says, "Recognize the unique position that He has placed you in."

Verily I say unto you, Whatsoever ye shall bind on earth shall be bound in heaven: and whatsoever ye shall loose on earth shall be loosed in heaven.
—Matthew 18:18

Every time you issue a word of encouragement or a warning, for that matter, and those things play out just as you prescribed, that's *prophetic revelation* and proof positive that the hand of God is working on your behalf. Paul says for that very reason, "Don't be shy, use that gift knowing whose gift it is, and you just might be one of the forerunners of greater things to come."

Every good gift and every perfect gift is from above, and cometh down from the Father of lights, with whom is no variableness, neither shadow of turning. Of his own will begat he us with the word of truth, that we should be a kind of firstfruits of his creatures.
—James 1:17–18

Now, in order to truly appreciate what God has determined to be our portion, one must first be willing to concede to our need to develop what I call triple vision.

•

- Hindsight, where the Father, through past events, shows His purpose and design.
- Insight, by which, through Christ's prophetic forecast, we can see His teachings being played out in today's world.
- Foresight, the insightful move of the Spirit, reveals those things that have yet to take place.

This is the only way we can offer up to God total praise. An historic praise for the things He's done. A right-now praise for the things He's doing, and a prophetic praise for those things we know He's going to do.

Until now, I didn't realize the intense role that prophecy, with all of its particulars being explicitly spelled out through the Bible, our road map and blueprint to success, would play in this generation. Through its guidance, we have seen how the ancients were able to recognize certain symbols and their prophetic value. God has led me to do extensive research and to seek out symbols that have long been used by wise men and prophets, which, according to the Scriptures, are now being made available to us today.

> Who can find a virtuous woman? for her price is far above rubies. . . . She maketh herself coverings of tapestry; her clothing is silk and purple.
> —Proverbs 31:10, 22

By way of prophetic applications, possibly through a dream or vision, these kinds of symbols can be found and recognized as timely revelations, such as in this narrative of the virtuous woman.

A woman generally reflects something that is both passive and alluring but must rise above being used or suffering loss. Jewelry (or rubies) commands attention and connotes that an important decision must be made, one that will determine the success of an event in the future. Purple is seen as neutral but also suggests that a negative situation is overcome by a positive action. All the attributes fall in line with this woman's life.

> *When they had heard the king, they departed; and, lo, the star, which they saw in the east, went before them, till it came and stood over where the young child was.*
> —Matthew 2:9

A star in a dream represents a symbol of friendship; dreams and hopes are about to materialize.

> *And she brought forth her firstborn son, and wrapped him in swaddling clothes, and laid him in a manger; because there was no room for them in the inn.*
> —Luke 2:7

The birth of a child speaks of innocence, childhood trust, and concerns. Warmth and new beginnings are also a part of this profile. The swaddling clothes represent someone who is taking on a role that possibly belonged to someone else. In this instance, a king for a king.

> *If any of you lack wisdom, let him ask of God, that giveth to all men liberally.*
> —James 1:5 KJV

But can the finite truly see into and understand the infinite, and how can the mind of a man comprehend the mind of God? The apostle Paul, a man inspired by the Spirit of God, put it this way:

> *This is why I, Paul, am in jail for Christ, having taken up the cause of you outsiders, so-called. I take it that you're familiar with the part I was given in God's plan for including everybody. I got the inside story on this from God himself, as I just wrote you in brief. As you read over what I have written to you, you'll be able to see for yourselves into the mystery of Christ. None of our ancestors understood this. Only in our time has it been made clear by God's Spirit through his holy apostles and prophets of this new order. The mystery is that people who have*

never heard of God and those who have heard of him all their lives (what I've been calling outsiders and insiders) stand on the same ground before God. They get the same offer, same help, same promises in Christ Jesus. The Message is accessible and welcoming to everyone, across the board. This is my life work: helping people understand and respond to this Message. It came as a sheer gift to me, a real surprise, God handling all the details. When it came to presenting the Message to people who had no background in God's way, I was the least qualified of any of the available Christians. God saw to it that I was equipped, but you can be sure that it had nothing to do with my natural abilities. And so here I am, preaching and writing about things that are way over my head, the inexhaustible riches and generosity of Christ. My task is to bring out in the open and make plain what God, who created all this in the first place, has been doing in secret and behind the scenes all along. Through followers of Jesus like yourselves gathered in churches, this extraordinary plan of God is becoming known and talked about even among the angels!

Ephesians 3:1–10 MSG

In these verses, Paul explains that everyone used of God is selected totally by His choice and at His discretion...His alone.

Ye have not chosen me, but I have chosen you, and ordained you, that ye should go and bring forth fruit, and that your fruit should remain.
—John 15:16

God had given him a special revelation and stewardship. He makes it clear that this was not something that he himself had earned, no more than you or I could earn our place in the Kingdom of God. It is a gift, and the proper response from one receiving such a grand gift would be to simply say "thank You," in this case through prayer, praise, and worship. I have learned to accept the fact that my journey, as with the journey of all men, was well-orchestrated, one that began in the womb of my mother and continues to be fostered and perpetuated to this very day. Now, one might ask what of those lives that have been cut short or have been wrongly or unjustly taken, because the feeling is that they have also suffered loss. But I believe even these events are there to impact the thinking and attitudes of those of us who are left behind. It has been said that "one moment with God in heaven is far greater than a lifetime with men on earth."

For a day in thy courts is better than a thousand.
—Psalm 84:10

The basic idea of this work is that it might be seen as a call to arms and to offer what I have termed the three *essentials*:

- Enlightenment, an introduction to the truth;
- Encouragement offers promise, purpose, and direction; and
- Empowerment, the strength from God to continue along this path.

We must be willing to assist those who might be grappling with the demon of confusion, as mankind's biggest frustration is to find the answers to questions like "Why am I here?" and "Whose idea was this anyway?" Many have turned to religion, only to end up feeling more confused and betrayed. Christianity has been blamed for causing a degree of uncertainty in so many lives. Small wonder, since it is evident to many observers that the Church herself has become fragmented. That's because the Church has been drawn into a compliant mindset. It's long been determined that most folks, both men and women, are the sum total of their life's experience. Their opinions and imaginations are based on the roads that life has taken them down. And without a concise word from God, it becomes easier for them to be swayed into bewilderment. To consolidate and fortify their power, the oligarchs who seek total domination aim to replace those vital ingredients of the Church with rigid, controlling doctrines or mandates that function as substitutes for religion. But just as there can be no life without blood pumping through one's body, there can be no cohesiveness or singleness of mind for the present-day Church without the direction and heart of God.

> *Keep thy heart with all diligence; for out of it are the issues of life.*
>
> —Proverbs 4:23

The truth is that Christianity is not responsible for the Church's dilemma, but it's the way Christianity has been misrepresented that constitutes the real problem. Our biggest battle is with what is called "secular humanism," a system of doctrines and practices that disregards or rejects any form of religious faith and worship. Many reject the idea of a superior mind being responsible for the existence of man, but when I look at the magnificent creatures, the tremendous design and the brilliant colors, the birds and fish that only flock and spawn together, when I look at man and his ability to manifest so many emotions and ideas, to be able to build, conquer, plan, and create, I refuse to accept the assessment of some person who one day stood up, put his thumbs under his suspenders, and announced,

"After careful consideration, I have determined that there is no God," and that we are all here as the result of some freak happening or cosmic collision. I tell you this: I would have gladly stood before that man and all who supported him and put my thumbs under my own suspenders—if I had some—and declared, "There are millions of us who have some say in this matter, and you have got to be out of your philosophical mind to think that we would allow all that we are and all that we might become to be summed up in your human opinion." Whenever I am confronted with the question of Darwin's Big Bang Theory, I always respond with three questions of my own:

- Who or what were the participants in this grand event?
- What force moved them into action?
- Where did it come from?

I will continue to proclaim to the world that we are not the result of some unforeseen event, but we are the result of divine excellence, and our Creator God is the mastermind of it all.

> *Behold, I am the LORD, the God of all flesh: is there any thing too hard for me?*
> —Jeremiah 32:27

CHAPTER 1

The God of Increase

The heavens declare the glory of God; and the firmament sheweth his handywork.

—Psalm 19:1

And so it begins, our amazing journey into the awesome plan and mind of God, just as He promised.

Remember ye not the former things, neither consider the things of old. Behold, I will do a new thing; now it shall spring forth; shall ye not know it? I will even make a way in the wilderness, and rivers in the desert.

—Isaiah 43:18–19

With His announcement of this *new thing*, God is saying, "Get ready to advance on new territories and be introduced to new horizons, where rivers, which represent the flow of the Spirit, will overtake the eerie dark-

ness of the wilderness and the dryness of the desert."
God will introduce a new and revealing insight of His
Word so that we might know and be fully prepared.

*He that believeth on me, as the scripture hath said, out of
his belly shall flow rivers of living water.*
—John 7:38

From here on, in order to launch this astonishing
sojourn, our first step must be toward His breathtak-
ing design—a design that in and of itself is beyond human comprehension. At the onset, there is nothing in
our region but God. Then He speaks, and it's on, and it's
beautiful and good.

In the beginning God created the heaven and the earth.
—Genesis 1:1

But that's just the beginning...in the next movement
of Scripture, we're introduced to the first created being
on earth, man.

*And God said, Let us make man in our image, af-
ter our likeness: and let them have dominion over
the fish of the sea, and over the fowl of the air, and
over the cattle, and over all the earth, and over every
creeping thing that creepeth upon the earth. So God*

created man in his own image, in the image of God created he him; male and female created he them.
—Genesis 1:26–27

Science tells us that for every action, there is a reaction. God's spoken words, "Let there be light," were the action, and the formation of all creations was the reaction to His command. For every cause, there is an effect; God was the cause, and man was the effect.

One would think that this unmatched display of design and creativity would be enough, but it wasn't over yet. To all of this beauty, bountifulness, and splendor, God adds a wrinkle. Another player, this dark force that would act as a disputant, attacker, assailant, a gamester, adversary, an antagonist called Lucifer. First, he shows up in the garden as a serpent.

Now the serpent was more subtil than any beast of the field which the LORD God had made. And he said unto the woman, Yea, hath God said, Ye shall not eat of every tree of the garden?
—Genesis 3:1

But later, he is formally introduced to us by the Old Testament prophets Isaiah and Ezekiel.

How art thou fallen from heaven, O Lucifer, son of the morning! how art thou cut down to the ground, which didst weaken the nations!

—Isaiah 14:12

Thou hast been in Eden the garden of God; every precious stone was thy covering, the sardius, topaz, and the diamond, the beryl, the onyx, and the jasper, the sapphire, the emerald, and the carbuncle, and gold: the workmanship of thy tabrets and of thy pipes was prepared in thee in the day that thou wast created. Thou art the anointed cherub that covereth; and I have set thee so: thou wast upon the holy mountain of God; thou hast walked up and down in the midst of the stones of fire. Thou wast perfect in thy ways from the day that thou wast created, till iniquity was found in thee.

Ezekiel 28:13–15

In an attempt to try to get a handle on this incredible procreation, let us now fast-forward into the future.

After this I beheld, and, lo, a great multitude, which no man could number, of all nations, and kindreds, and people, and tongues, stood before the throne, and before the Lamb, clothed with white robes, and palms in their hands; And cried with a loud voice, saying, Salvation to our God which sitteth upon the throne, and unto the Lamb.

—Revelation 7:9–10

Here in the book of Revelation, we get a glimpse into eternity, where an untold number of people are voluntarily praising God in response to some unforgettable feat that He had performed in their lives. So, we have the beginning, and we have the ending. The only thing left is the strategy in the middle, complete with its checks and balances, which later would be referred to as light against darkness, right against wrong, and good against evil. But through it all, God would leave no doubt as to who the Architect of this entire universal system was.

> *I form the light, and create darkness: I make peace, and create evil: I the LORD do all these things. Drop down, ye heavens, from above, and let the skies pour down righteousness: let the earth open, and let them bring forth salvation, and let righteousness spring up together; I the LORD have created it*
> —Isaiah 45:7–8

This proclamation from Jehovah Elohim (the Creator) makes it unanimously clear: *"I the LORD do all these things"* (verse 7). No matter how it may appear that God's plan for His chosen people has been derailed, in reality, nothing could be further from the truth. Even though the Church may not currently be walking in all that's been assigned her, God's gifts are without repentance.

No man can claim to know all there is to know about God. It would be a fundamental impossibility. However, He has given us enough to assemble a comprehensive picture of what His intentions are and the vastness of His being. One thing is certain: Nothing can sidetrack any purpose or plan that God has set in motion before the foundation of this world. It doesn't matter how many obstacles it might face or how many challenges must be met; whenever God issues a decree, it will ultimately come to pass.

The stage has long been set to bring true believers into a oneness, first with themselves, their brethren, and eventually, with their Creator God. At the root of all of this, God has set in place both an idea and a solution. The idea is *love*; the solution is *blood*.

This is the entire idea.

For all the law is fulfilled in one word, even in this; Thou shalt love thy neighbor as thyself.
—Galatians 5:14

This is the entire solution.

For the life of the flesh is in the blood: and I have given it to you upon the altar to make an atonement for your souls: for it is the blood that maketh an atonement for the soul.

—Leviticus 17:11

Consider these words written by the apostle Paul showing that in our moving forward, He (God) is no respecter of persons, but is the designer and benefactor of all gifts.

For when the Gentiles, which have not the law, do by nature the things contained in the law, these, having not the law, are a law unto themselves.

—Romans 2:14

This Scripture confirms that God works from the inside out, and it is His Spirit that implements the process by which a person can be transformed from rags to riches or rubble to righteousness. This includes the gifts of discernment and revelations that will come to the dreamers and visionaries of this day. The same Spirit that leads and guides also introduces a yoke-breaking word, allowing the oppressed to face down those things that have held them in bondage, things such as fear, hatred, prejudice, indifference, or unforgiveness.

That word, I say, ye know, which was published throughout all Judaea, and began from Galilee, after the baptism which John preached; How God anointed Jesus of Nazareth with the Holy Ghost and with power: who went about doing good, and healing all that were oppressed of the devil; for God was with him.

—Acts 10:37–38

We have been given our release from the God of Increase. "To increase" is "to grow in size, degree, or amount, to multiply by producing offspring." These words were spoken to the patriarch Abraham in the book of Genesis.

That in blessing I will bless thee, and in multiplying I will multiply thy seed as the stars of the heaven, and as the sand which is upon the sea shore; and thy seed shall possess the gate of his enemies.

—Genesis 22:17

Abraham, we are told, was willing to offer up to God as a blood sacrifice his beloved son, Isaac. God's response to this unselfish act was to promise, *"That in blessing I will bless thee, and in multiplying I will multiply thy seed as the stars of the heaven..."* (verse 17).

The fact that God has much to offer and the right and authority to do so is exemplified in the Old Testament book of Psalms:

But our God is in the heavens: he hath done whatsoever he hath pleased.

—Psalm 115:3

The implication here is that all one must do is lift up their head on a star-filled night and gaze into what is obviously infinity. And if there was some doubt or question about God's vastness or His greatness, that particular issue should be resolved, as we are admonished by another Old Testament psalm that says, *"The fool hath said in his heart, There is no God..."* (Psalm 14:1).

If there is a God, then surely He has a plan and a time for that plan to be executed. No matter how radical it may appear to be to some, it is more than obvious that the time is now, and the plan has been set before us. This huge drama has been in the making for a long, long time, from the smallest minute detail to the grandest of all scales.

All flesh is not the same flesh: but there is one kind of flesh of men, another flesh of beasts, another of fishes, and another of birds. There are also celestial bodies and bodies terrestrial: but the glory of the celestial is one, and the glory of the terrestrial is another. There is one glory of the sun, and another glory of the moon, and another glory of the stars: for one star differeth from another star in glory.

—1 Corinthians 15:39–41

No one knows how long this has been going on but estimates for some older star clusters range from fifty million to ten billion years and beyond. The larger of these being called the Andromeda Galaxy, and all of this is just a tiny fraction of what our God is working on. (Hallelujah!) Now during this, in our immediate neighborhood, an area called an inner solar system about ninety-three million miles from its one sun orbits the third planet, Earth. Like Mercury, Venus, and Mars, Earth is a terrestrial world, a solid sphere made mostly of silicates and metals. It is the largest-known example of this class of planet. It is unlike any other in its composition, its climate, and its support of life as we know and understand it.

Earth's blessed atmosphere traps just the right amount of solar energy to raise the ground temperature comfortably above the freezing point of water. Its distance from the sun allows for conditions that are conducive to the presence of liquid surface water. These two factors ensure that well over two-thirds of our planet's surface is covered with water. This is the key to

Earth's ability to be an incubator of life. If it were slightly cooler or hotter, the water would have frozen solid or else evaporated a long time ago, and without water to refresh us, where would mankind be?

Now for the best part: Our planet, Earth, is enshrouded, or covered, if you will, in a blanket of ionized gas called plasmasphere or plasma, which is the same name given to the liquid portion of blood.

Curiously, it seems that the idea of a blood covering has always been ushered to the forefront of man's thinking as part of God's universal plan.

That's why some of us get so excited when we read Scriptures like those found in the book of Psalms.

Many, O LORD my God, are thy wonderful works which thou hast done, and thy thoughts which are to us-ward: they cannot be reckoned up in order unto thee: if I would declare and speak of them, they are more than can be numbered.

—Psalm 40:5

He telleth the number of the stars; he calleth them all by their names. Great is our Lord, and of great power: his understanding is infinite.

—Psalm 147:4–5

We stand in total agreement with the writer of these Psalms, who is captivated and swept away by the idea that this all-powerful, all-knowing God, perfect and present God, is our God. And that this God for whom there are no formulas or devices to measure His fullness has thoughts about us. We are always on His infinitely divine mind. Just think, all those stars, and He is not only able to call them out—that is, to create them—but He is also able to name them one by one.

This speaks not only to His ability, but to His willingness as well to interact with that which He has created. This is a tremendous commodity, knowing that as we advance, we are never without the protection, strength, and guidance of El-Shaddai (God Almighty) and His love toward us.

When thou goest, it shall lead thee; when thou sleepest, it shall keep thee; and when thou awakest, it shall talk with thee.
—Proverbs 6:22

CHAPTER 2

Seeing through the Eyes of Promise

Behold, I will do a new a thing; now it shall spring forth; shall ye not know it? I will even make a way in the wilderness, and rivers in the desert. The beast of the field shall honour me, the dragons and the owls: because I give waters in the wilderness, and rivers in the desert, to give drink to my people, my chosen. This people have I formed for myself; they shall shew forth my praise.

Isaiah 43:19–21

This prophetic window and others like it peering into the future of God's chosen remains a perplexing enigma to the people of God and to those who have been introduced to their predetermined destiny. They are often left with more questions than answers. Questions like "When and how is all this supposed to take place?" As always, God remains true to His tradition, as He continues to keep men in suspense until He is ready to reveal His handiwork. According to what we have learned, those revelations will come from people who have been endowed with God's spirit of prophecy. That is why we should never take our eyes off of the limitless possibilities of *The Infinite Being, God*, Him whom we worship.

But the path of the just is as the shining light, that shineth more and more.

—Proverbs 4:18

We know that there are certain types who will be appalled at the idea that, as the Church, we would have the audacity to think somehow, and in some way, we should get involved with mankind's horrific situations. However, we are of the *Ecclesia*—"a called-out remnant" that God has set in place and in motion for this point in time. Moreover, our being part of this remnant gives us every right to speak in the way that we do, confidently and uninhibited. We are genuinely concerned with the prosperity and well-being of those around us. It is by God's Holy Spirit that we feel compelled to issue this prophetic clarion call to all we encounter, that it is time (God's time) for a new thing.

God that made the world and all things therein, seeing that he is Lord of heaven and earth, dwell-

eth not in temples made with hands; neither is wor-
shipped with men's hands, as though he needed any
thing, seeing he giveth to all life, and breath, and
all things; and hath made of one blood all nations
of men for to dwell on all the face of the earth, and
hath determined the times before appointed, and
the bounds of their habitation.

Acts 17:24–26

Just as we are familiar with the term "landlord"
as describing a property owner who leases his property to others, so is God the Lord of both heaven and
earth. Therefore, He should not be minimized in our
thoughts toward Him. So often, because of the volumi-
nous boundless stature of God, for many, it is difficult
to imagine the very mind, attention, and design of Him
trickling down into and becoming interwoven with
the concerns of mortal men, not just at some particular event or juncture in their lives, but from the very
moment of their inception. Paul shares with us the
definitive linkage that God has with men and the common linkage that men have with each other—*one blood.*

Paul is very confident and comfortable with the idea
that when it comes to God's created being, man, every
step that he makes, every breath that he takes, every
inch of ground that he covers, and every person that he

meets have all been measured, appointed, and determined before time ever was.

When I look back at what appeared to be a mundane existence and life that began without real purpose, I am thoroughly amazed at the fact that God was always around, which is to say, "No matter how dismal or grim an event or circumstance may appear to be, there has never been a moment or place in time where God was not in attendance."

And Moses said unto God, Who am I, that I should go unto Pharaoh, and that I should bring forth the children of Israel out of Egypt?

—Exodus 3:11

Who am I to accept this call? Moses found himself confronted with challenges that he felt exceeded his ability to perform. Who would have thought that after forty years of living in exile, this man, Moses, born of Hebrew slaves and, at the time of this particular event, a fugitive in hiding, would be used of God to deliver his people, Israel, out of Egyptian bondage? At least in Moses' mind, this task that he had been summoned to undertake was both huge and unthinkable. Just look at what this man was called to do.

At Israel's birth, Egypt had already had many centuries of stable national life behind her. The Pharaohs were not only the lords of a dynasty; they were also the

patrons of a majestic culture. The pyramids and hiero-
glyphic inscriptions on walls and tombs showed their
intense ambition to preserve and transmit the Egyptian
experience. Massive statues and exquisite mural paint-
ings reflect their artistic imaginations. The political
sway of Egypt's strength and power ran from the Nile,
which is in Sudan, across the Sinai wilderness into
Canaan and Syria. Sometimes an Egyptian expedition
would reach as far westward as Libya. Moses was born
at a time when the Pharaoh, the ruler of Egypt—a most
powerful and magnificent dynasty—had given orders
that no more male Hebrew children should be allowed
to live. The Hebrew slaves had been reproducing so fast
that he felt threatened by a Hebrew revolt against his
authority. But to save her young child's life, his mother
fashioned a basket of papyrus, waterproofed it with as-
phalt and pitch, and set it afloat on the Nile River. By
God's divine providence, the child was recovered by a
princess who was the daughter of Pharaoh and would
raise him as her own son.

However, unbeknownst to the princess in her search
to find a nursemaid to rear the child, she chose Moses'
own mother, who would play a critical role and have
tremendous influence in the life of this young prince of
Egypt. Moses' forty years in Egypt afforded him ample
time to learn many things concerning the Egyptian culture and way of life. Also, I believe, at some point dur-

ing that same time, he struggled with his innermost feelings concerning the accepted practices of how the Jews, then called Hebrews, were to be treated. In a fit of anger, Moses took the life of an Egyptian soldier for beating a Hebrew slave, and this led to his banishment from the land.

The Bible's depiction of Moses' first encounter with God makes it apparent that his approach to *"this great sight"* (a burning bush) was that of a curious observer. Little did he know that he was being led down a path that God had set in place for him long before he was ever born.

> *Remember the former things of old: for I am God,*
> *and there is none else; I am God, and there is none*
> *like me, declaring the end from the beginning, and*
> *from ancient times the things that are not yet done,*
> *saying, My counsel shall stand, and I will do all my*
> *pleasure.*
>
> Isaiah 46:9–10

I can certainly connect with Moses' dilemma during that time. His feelings of compassion were born out of a place that was not easily identifiable, and his feelings of frustration derived from knowing what should be done but not knowing exactly how to do it. But in his dilemma, what he received was a prophetic mantle from God, which was something that he would eventually become familiar with. In another place under God's direction, Moses gathered seventy elders of the people and set them around the tabernacle. Upon doing so, God took of the spirit of prophecy that was upon Moses and gave it to the elders, and they began to prophesy. However, there were two men that were not of that group, but the Spirit rested upon them as well, and they, too, began to prophesy. Believing that these men were out of place, a young man reported the incident to Moses. Moses' response was not only to sanction his actions but also to inform him that God has the right to place His spirit upon whomsoever He pleases.

> And there ran a young man, and told Moses, and said, Eldad and Medad do prophecy in the camp. And Joshua the son of Nun, the servant of Moses, one of his young men, answered and said, My lord Moses, forbid them. And Moses said unto him, Enviest thou for my sake? would God that all the LORD's people were prophets, and the LORD would put his spirit upon them!
>
> —Numbers 11:27–29

> And now we are rising from the ashes, and we are putting forth our hands; look inside us for our story, see through our eyes and understand.
>
> —A gift from an Indian friend

The reason why I shared this striking antidote is that, as a people, at least up to this point, we are still divided in the Church. While on the other hand, the final unification of God's prophetic Church has been in the works throughout the ages, all-encompassed by a vision of descent from a single ancestor. Remember *"one blood."* The narrative in Genesis of Abraham, Isaac, and Jacob is presented in the language of ecclesiastic pride. It evokes the memory of an age in which God walked intimately with men and intervened in the daily commerce of their lives. A spiritually inspired Moses chronicles this biblical account; we are told that Abraham received divine instructions to leave his land and kinsmen for a new country, where he would be awarded a historic lineage of his own. One that God would place squarely on the shoulders of Christ and those who would later be led by His spirit.

For unto us a child is born, unto us a son is given: and the government shall be upon his shoulder: and his name shall be called Wonderful, Counsellor, The mighty God, The everlasting Father, The Prince of Peace.
—Isaiah 9:6

All of this was set in place as a brilliant snapshot of things to come.

For whom he did foreknow, he also did predesti-
nate to be conformed to the image of his Son, that
he might be the firstborn among many brethren.
Moreover whom he did predestinate, them he also
called: and whom he called, them he also justified:
and whom he justified, them he also glorified.
What shall we then say to these things? If God be
for us, who can be against us?

—Romans 8:29–31

For by one Spirit are we all baptized into one body, whether
we be Jews or Gentiles, whether we be bond or free; and have
been all made to drink into one Spirit.

—1 Corinthians 12:13

It's a fact that people from all spheres of life are feel-ing what I am saying now. We are all here because God deposited us here, and we need to follow Him and His plan for this hour. The apostle Paul makes it clear that this end-time spiritual surge *will fall* upon believers as well as those who are currently unbelievers.

In Matthew 13, Jesus recites a parable concerning tares and wheat being planted in the same garden, and the servants of the sower offered to separate the two based on their own judgments.

But he said, Nay; lest while ye gather up the tares, ye root up also the wheat with them.

—Matthew 13:29

This is what Paul calls the one body being made to drink of the one Spirit.

Take my yoke upon you, and learn of me; for I am meek and lowly in heart: and ye shall find rest unto your souls.

—Matthew 11:29

Through the Scriptures, we are admonished to hold our schools of thought concerning God and His Christ until we have first given them the benefit of learning who they really are. These words were written by the Old Testament prophet Jeremiah.

And ye shall seek me, and find me, when ye shall search for me with all your heart.

—Jeremiah 29:13

We are encouraged to take this unchartered journey that will ultimately bring us face-to -face with God. The only criteria are that we have a sincere desire to know Him and to learn what He had in mind for our lives when He commissioned us to be here. I want my friends to see this as a journey through the eyes of promise, where an ordinary man, one who was drawn to God by His truths and His truths alone, was given a desire to get closer to a grand idea, one that might someday and in some way, help bridge the gap between the here and the hereafter and rectify the long-awaited union between the human and the divine.

CHAPTER 3

When God is Not Enough

In our opening chapter, we had identified one who would be the father of all lies and negative thoughts. From his very beginning, Satan had set out to change God's plans and implement his own. Little did he know, as we follow his antics, that he would remain a pawn in the hands of He who created him.

Who changed the truth of God into a lie, and worshipped and served the creature more than the Creator, who is blessed for ever. Amen.

—Romans 1:25

Every attack waged in his attempt to influence and weaken the minds of men would only serve as just another phase, or stepping-stone, added to the Church's history and this huge majestic Kingdom that God is building for Himself and those who are called by His name. That's why it's imperative that we keep a keen eye on this enemy of life, liberty, and truth, as he continues in his quest to deceive mankind with his bedeviling devices.

Lest Satan should get an advantage of us: for we are not ignorant of his devices.

—2 Corinthians 2:11

And the Lord spake unto Moses that selfsame day, saying, Get thee up into this mountain Abarim, unto mount Nebo, which is in the land of Moab, that is over against Jericho; and behold the land of Canaan, which I give unto the children of Israel for a possession: And die in the mount whither thou goest up, and be gathered unto thy people; as Aaron thy brother died in mount Hor, and was gathered unto his people.

—Deuteronomy 32:48–50

This passage in Deuteronomy heralds the close of one era and the beginning of another. Moses had served out his duration as prophet, deliverer, leader, and lawgiver of the Hebrew people. During his period as a leader, Moses was so inspired by God that he was able to build a united nation among a race of oppressed and weary slaves. But Moses would eventually succumb to the wants and desires of his people rather than the desires of God. It had become evident to Moses at this point in their pilgrimage that their faith was waning, and for some, overtly trusting in God was not enough.

At the close of this movement, Moses had only one more task to fulfill before ascending Mount Nebo, where he would take his last breath. His final assignment was to bless the children of Israel. He would then gaze over into a land flowing with milk and honey for the first and last time, a land that he himself would not be allowed to enter; this land was called Canaan. Under the leadership of Moses, the Hebrews had endured an arduous journey through the desert to reach Canaan. It was here that the first kings—Saul, David, and Solomon—created the kingdom of Israel.

This land remained of fundamental importance to its people throughout its traditional history and subsequently the history of the Church as well: its division into rival kingdoms of Israel and Judah, their fall to the Assyrians and Babylonians, the exile of the people of Judah, and their return to the land ruled successively by Persia, Greece, and Rome.

Then all the elders of Israel gathered themselves together, and came to Samuel unto Ramah, and said unto him, Behold, thou art old, and thy sons walk not in thy ways: now make us a king to judge us like all the nations.

—1 Samuel 8:4–5

It is a forgone conclusion that God is never slacking concerning His promises. It's only when we set out to take matters into our own hands that we often end up digging a hole for ourselves that only He can get us out of.

And the LORD said unto Samuel, Hearken unto the voice of the people in all that they say unto thee: for they have not rejected thee, but they have rejected me, that I should not reign over them.

—1 Samuel 8:7

Under demonic influence, the people had made up their minds that they no longer wanted to serve this invisible God; they wanted someone they could see, touch, and hear an audible voice. They wanted a man who could sit tall on a horse and go before them in battle. Samuel, the last judge of Israel, tried to warn them of the consequences of having a man rather than the God that delivered them out of Egypt to reign over them. We must be careful not to get too comfortable with the idea of placing any one person above the dictates or designs of Him who set it all in place.

The earth is the LORD's, and the fulness thereof; the world, and they that dwell therein. For he hath founded it upon the seas, and established it upon the floods. Who shall ascend into the hill of the LORD? Or who shall stand in his holy place?

—Psalm 24:1–3

Like many who have gone before us, we must never forget that our God is a God of progression. Every event is linked in some way to those things that will be next in succession to it. Our God is a multifaceted wonder; that's why we are told that His voice is like the voice of "many waters" (Psalm 29:3). If we follow Him closely, we can see how He has hewed out a clear path from natural creation to eternal salvation. It was never intended to be a one-man show, but with every segment being fitly joined together. The voices of God's continuing prophecies have not yet been silenced. There is still much to be said.

Behold, the former things are come to pass, and new things do I declare: before they spring forth I tell you of them.

—Isaiah 42:9

God always has and always will have definitive voices to project the next round of events moving forward, those who were to demonstrate what God called *His new thing,* being led by His Spirit through dreams and visions.

This people have I formed for myself; they shall show forth my praise.

—Isaiah 43:21

However, because these people did not heed the warnings of God's prophet to understand that theirs was just another link in a long chain, they remained adamant; their minds were made up because this is what happens to men when God is not enough.

Nevertheless the people refused to obey the voice of Samuel; and they said, Nay; but we will have a king over us; that we also may be like all the nations; and that our king may judge us, and go out before us, and fight our battles.

—1 Samuel 8:19–20

They had forgotten what it was like to draw breath and thrive under the protection of God's Shekinah Glory. They had also forgotten about those times when they would lift Him up in praise, how they themselves would be lifted up above the frightful and threatening demands that so often confronted them.

Let me make it clear that this observation is in no way intended to level an indictment against the people of God. I believe that at its core, Israel loved God, but like so many before and after her, they were unable to relinquish their will for His. This left them juggling loyalties and trying to glean the best of both worlds...the world of righteousness under the Law of Moses, and the world of the uncircumcised Gentiles that was filled with folly, kings, and idols.

Whoso despiseth the word shall be destroyed: but he that feareth the commandment shall be rewarded. The law of the wise is a fountain of life, to depart from the snares of death.
—Proverbs 13:13–14

This proverb was written by King Solomon, the king who acquired the reputation of being the wisest man that ever lived. Following the death of Solomon and the ensuing division of the kingdom, Israel on the north and Judah on the south, Israel's link to Jerusalem was broken. A duality of military campaigns against them ensued, first by the Assyrians in 732 BC. As the empire of the Assyrians declined, its powerful east rival Babylon grew in strength. The kingdom of Judah was caught in the struggle of the two and Egypt's attempts to intervene. The Babylonians defeated the Assyrians, drove out the Egyptians, and created a vast new empire. They twice invaded Judah and annexed the Israelite kingdom. After the attack of Jerusalem in 586 BC, they carried off its leading citizens into exile in Babylon. The destruction of Jerusalem and its temple by the Babylonians and the enforced journey into Babylon of the exiled Jews left them feeling that they had been abandoned by God.

This precarious position that Israel found herself in gave rise to many of the prophetic inferences that would shed even more light on what God's true motives were.

And there shall come forth a rod out of the stem of Jesse, and a Branch shall grow out of his roots: And the spirit of the LORD shall rest upon him, the spirit of wisdom and understanding, the spirit of counsel and might, the spirit of knowledge and the fear of the LORD.

—Isaiah 11:1–2

Behold, the days come saith the LORD, that I will raise unto David a righteous Branch, and a King shall reign and prosper, and shall execute judgment and justice in the earth. In his days Judah shall be saved, and Israel shall dwell safely: and this is his name whereby he shall be called, THE LORD OUR RIGHTEOUSNESS.

—Jeremiah 23:5–6

Through the prophets Isaiah and Jeremiah, God assured them that they, His children, His chosen, would eventually return with renewed faith to the God of their fathers. This guarantee would be repeated over and over again by reminding them that no matter what men might do to them, Israel's God would always be there.

Not only that, but God offered His forecast for a brilliant future filled with endless possibilities.

And afterward they desired a king: and God gave unto them Saul the son of Cis, a man of the tribe of Benjamin, by the space of forty years. And when he had removed him, he raised up unto them David to be their king; to whom also he gave their testimony, and said, I have found David the son of Jesse, a man after mine own heart, which shall fulfill all my will. Of this man's seed hath God according to his promise raised unto Israel a Saviour, Jesus.

Acts 13:21–23

Of course, all these things are rehearsed in our minds and in our spirits so that we might understand that every single one of those events was to lead us down a faithful path toward God's grand finale.

Therefore thus saith the Lord GOD, Behold, I lay in Zion for a foundation a stone, a tried stone, a precious corner stone, a sure foundation: he that believeth shall not make haste.

—Isaiah 28:16

For other foundation can no man lay than that is laid, which is Jesus Christ.

—1 Corinthians 3:11

Our marching orders are clear; understanding that the work is not yet finished, we are to continue down those corridors that have already been laid out for us.

Follow after charity, and desire spiritual gifts, but rather that ye may prophesy.
—1 Corinthians 14:1

Now he that planteth and he that watereth are one: and every man shall receive his own reward according to his own labour. For we are labourers together with God: ye are God's husbandry, ye are God's building.
—1 Corinthians 3:8–9

And so it is, the whole account of Israel's history up to this point is, in fact, a testament of God's faithfulness to His blood covenants. Whatever God signs in blood will remain intact, no matter what the party or parties on the other side of the agreement might do.

This chapter was not written to highlight the downside of human nature or man's inability to work in union with God. On the contrary, it is to place a strong emphasis on God's determination to work in union with man, to prove that when it comes to meeting our needs, He is more than adequate.

Not that we are sufficient of ourselves to think any thing as of ourselves; but our sufficiency is of God.

—2 Corinthians 3:5

Once God has decreed a certain thing, it's never a matter of if, but with Him, it's simply a matter of when. We know that there are many who promote the doctrine of abandonment by the inference that God bailed out on Israel when they needed Him most.

They continue to fan the flame by asking the question, what happened to the covenant that promised prosperity and protection? The events of Israel's past clearly show that God, like a devout father, even when His children were oblivious to His motives, was always teaching. The lesson that was to be learned is how easily we can fall prey to the aggressions of our enemies or adversaries when Him whom we worship—*God*—is not enough.

CHAPTER 4

Blood is Thicker Than Water

For the LORD will pass through to smite the Egyptians; and when he seeth the blood upon the lintel, and on the two side posts, the LORD will pass over the door, and will not suffer the destroyer to come in unto your houses to smite you. And ye shall observe this thing for an ordinance to thee and to thy sons for ever.

—Exodus 12:23–24

And as they were eating, Jesus took bread, and blessed it, and brake it, and gave it to the disciples, and said, Take, eat; this is my body. And he took the cup, and gave thanks, and gave it to them, saying, Drink ye all of it; For this is my blood of the new testament, which is shed for many for the remission of sins.

—Matthew 26:26–28

Now, if there is one indisputable fact of human existence, it is that no matter what one's ethnic persuasion, gender, or age might be, from the very beginning, blood has been the single common link that ties all of mankind together. God has placed a significant amount of entitlement in the blood, even more so with those who remain under His blood covenant.

From Genesis to Jesus, even unto this very day, the blood represents a crimson rope that intertwines the multicultural Christian Church into a perpetual oneness. Although the natural man may fade away and return to the dust, because of something as simple as the blood of a Passover lamb in Egypt and the tremendous act of love that was carried out on Calvary, these blood ties will remain forever.

On the surface, one would think that just having God's word of assurance would be enough for those who trust Him. But God also preordained that the solution to the believers' dejection would not just be in a promise alone but by a sacrificial oath and the actual spilling of life-giving blood.

When we look at the book of Exodus (Exodus 12:23–24), Israel was under an inescapable bondage because she had insisted for a time that God was not enough; she was being held fast by an adversary who briefly appeared invincible in every sense of the word. For over four hundred years, the Egyptians loomed over Israel like a dark cloud, and through Pharaoh, a force of evil was raging. Little did the people of Egypt know that God was going to turn a whole nation from being victims of an Egyptian dynasty into heirs of a victorious legacy. He would change the course of history, Church history, through something as simple as *the blood of a lamb*.

> *All we like sheep have gone astray; we have turned every one to his own way; and the LORD hath laid on him the iniquity of us all. He was oppressed, and he was afflicted, yet he opened not his mouth: he is brought as a lamb to the slaughter, and as a sheep before her shearers is dumb, so he openeth not his mouth. He was taken from prison and from judgment: and who shall declare his generation? for he was cut off out of the land of the living: for the transgression of my people was he stricken.*
> —Isaiah 53:6–8

All these things would have never been brought to light with such brilliance and intensity if not for the long-seeing eye of prophecy: "*...who shall declare his generation?*" God's Word of verification has always remained a staple to the continuing advancement of His divine timetable, as through His Word and by His Spirit, we can see how so many today will be called to the forefront of a predetermined agenda.

Now, I want you to take note that when the angel of death was given his orders, he was not told to take an inventory of anyone's life. This apparently was something that God was going to do later. And though all were not in place as far as their faith in God was concerned, because of who they were, *His chosen*, they remained covered by the blood.

For those who insist on being judgmental against Israel, let us not forget that God always knew what He was doing. He knew there would be many who were steeped in unbelief because of their suffering, but because blood is thicker than water, they didn't have to be perfect to be blessed.

For a long while, Israel's life was in the hands of a Pharaoh; however, there is nothing like God showing up in the middle of a crisis to bring about a change in the hearts of those who might doubt. For years, Israel's fate was in the hands of a man, but because of the blood, it would be recovered by a promise.

For when God made promise to Abraham, because he could swear by no greater, he sware by himself, saying, Surely blessing I will bless thee, and multiplying I will multiply thee.
—Hebrews 6:13–14

If the blood of a lamb could deliver a nation under a prior *Abrahamic covenant*, then certainly it is no small miracle that our lives are spared under this new covenant, one also consummated by blood.

For this is my blood of the new testament, which is shed for many for the remission of sins.
                                                    —Matthew 26:28

It is a foregone conclusion that every sin you or I have been indicted for, accused of, and found guilty of was already contemplated by Jehovah Elohim Jehovah (*I Am That I Am*). Jehovah Elohim Jehovah already knew the kinds of things that we could get into with the help of those satanic forces that surround us. Not only had God seen us, but He had already preordained a place and time for our deliverance and the instrument He would use to bring us out.

This is where the impossible becomes possible by grace. For all whose hearts are opened toward Him, the time is always right now; the place is where you are, and the instrument is still an old rugged cross so that we, too, like the Hebrews in Egypt, might be set free as we enter into a more perfect union. Additionally, through God's Spirit, we can gain deeper insight into the old family cliché that advances the notion "Blood is thicker than water." By the shedding of Christ's blood, God has called us to a higher plane. *Plane* is defined as "a surface that connects and carries a straight line joining any two points lying on it," the two points here being love and faith.

Having predestinated us unto the adoption of children by Jesus Christ to himself, according to the good pleasure of his will, to the praise of the glory of his grace, wherein he hath made us accepted in the beloved.

—Ephesians 1:5–6

God Himself has engrafted us into the Beloved and made us Mishpachah—family. This joining demands a higher or greater degree of adherence than most are willing to acknowledge. Our Father, who is in heaven, is indeed speaking to His people in more positive ways and will continue to do so because the continued advancement of the Great Commission is not yet over, but for some of us, it's just getting started.

That's why for those who are already blessed exceedingly and abundantly above all they can ask or think, there remains an even greater reason not to sit down on God. Nowhere in the Scriptures are we encouraged to seek out a comfortable spot where we can sit and wait for the rapture. Instead, we are told to be reaching, preaching, and teaching people that God is calling and empowering us, to continue in our quest to set before Him a reconciled church.

Being confident of this very thing, that he which hath be-gun a good work in you will perform it until the day of Jesus Christ.

—Philippians 1:6

The very essence of this Scripture causes me to have a problem accepting legalism in the church. In every society or organized group of people, two types are always recognized, those looking back to the past and the progressive looking forward to the future. I have yet to understand how traditionalist and newly enlightened Christians can be co-laborers. God is always calling us out of our comfort zones, showing up when we least expect Him, and asking us to do things our uncommitted lazy side does not normally want to do.

God is moving His Church to a new era—not one where we just sit content in an assembly, but instead, one where the church is so fired up they can't wait to get in the presence of their next target or potential convert.

God wants us to understand that this thing is a whole lot bigger than we are. He wants all of us to know that our very being goes a lot further than the person we see in the mirror every morning. His plan for us is more than that which meets the natural eye.

Why is blood thicker than water? It's by the remi-niscence of oneness that the blood corroborates. God will continue to shape, mold, and position His new covenant, raising us together, Jew and Gentile, as He prepares to present us to the entire world as one new man.

It is God who determined that the predominant solution to our coexistence, co-laboring, co-destiny with Him by way of the cross would be found in *the blood*.

> *Wherein God, willing more abundantly to shew unto the heirs of promise the immutability of his counsel, confirmed it by an oath: That by two immutable things, in which it was impossible for God to lie, we might have a strong consolation, who have fled for refuge to lay hold upon the hope set before us.*
>
> —Hebrews 6:17–18

CHAPTER 5

A New Covenant

But this shall be the covenant that I will make with the house of Israel; after those days, saith the LORD, I will put my law in their inward parts, and write it in their hearts; and will be their God, and they shall be my people. And they shall teach no more every man his neighbour, and every man his brother, saying, Know the LORD: for they shall all know me, from the least of them unto the greatest of them, saith the LORD: for I will forgive their iniquity, and I will remember their sin no more.
—Jeremiah 31:33–34

Through the Jewish prophet Jeremiah, God informs us of a new covenant that would be introduced in detail at a later time. *"After those days,"* this new covenant fixed in God's mind and purposed in His heart would be based solely on the counsel of His own sovereign will. In other words, the operative statement in Jeremiah's prophecy is, *"But this shall be the covenant that I will make..."*; there were no votes cast or opinions sought after concerning His decision. After reading Jeremiah's prophecy, one is left with the notion that this expansive plan would extend beyond the boundaries of race, creed, or color, *"...for they shall all know me..."* This makes perfectly good sense when we consider the fact that if there is but one God, a belief shared by Jews, Christians, and Muslims alike, then He would have to be the one and only Creator of all mankind. This would also mean that everyone was included in His plan and would therefore have some specific role to fulfill. It is imperative that we begin to take a look at both our selective and collective roles and prepare ourselves to boldly step into them.

Behold, I will send my messenger, and he shall prepare the way before me: and the LORD, whom ye seek, shall suddenly come to his temple, even the messenger of the covenant, whom ye delight in: behold, he shall come, saith the LORD of hosts.
—Malachi 3:1

Once again, God is speaking to us, this time using the prophet Malachi. He promises to send His messenger John the Baptist, who would be the frontrunner of Jesus Christ, another extremely confident and equally impressive messenger and interpreter of this new covenant.

44

But the hour cometh, and now is, when the true worship-pers shall worship the Father in spirit and in truth: for the Father seeketh such to worship him.

—John 4:23

This statement delineated by Christ not only re-counts a new covenant but also bears witness to God's reaching out to those sanctioned by His prophetic cov-ering, whose voices would denote truth as lights that would shine in dark places.

But the path of the just is as the shining light, that shineth more and more unto the perfect day.

—Proverbs 4:18

This speaks directly into the heart to a time of full-ness, which was to come, as it would be four hundred years between the close of the Old Testament with Mal-achi as its last prophet and the opening of the Christian or "common era" with Matthew. These would be known by many as the "silent years," as there appeared to be no open vision from God.

Behold, the days come, saith the Lord GOD, that I will send a famine in the land, not a famine of bread, nor a thirst for wa-ter, but of hearing the words of the LORD.

—Amos 8:11

Of course, all of this would be rescinded by way of God's infinite wisdom and His amazing grace. In this final hour through God's chosen from their fascinating vantage point, there will be that which represents a balm in Gilead.

Is there no balm in Gilead; is there no physician there? why then is not the health of the daughter of my people recovered?
—Jeremiah 8:22

From the refounding of the nation under Persian rule with Nehemiah and Ezra (444 BCE) to the savage overthrow of Jerusalem, the Judean capital, by the Roman general Pompeii, there remained an extremely powerful Jewish enthusiasm among the inhabitants of Judah. Always, there seemed to be this sense of a new day with brand new possibilities for Judah's independence. It created a strong belief that this independence loomed just around the corner.

But now hath he obtained a more excellent ministry, by how much also he is the mediator of a better covenant, which was established upon better promises. For if that first covenant had been faultless, then should no place have been sought for the second. For finding fault with them, he saith, Behold, the days come, saith the Lord, when I will make a new covenant with the house of Israel and with the house of Judah.

—Hebrews 8:6–8

At the birth of Christianity, the Jewish presence had already crossed the boundaries of Palestine. Jews had settled in almost all the countries in the civilized world. The name Palestine entered common usage during the Greco-Roman period, a period influenced by both Greeks and Romans. In the Bible, it was used to designate the country of the Philistines, a coastal stretch adjoining the Sharon Valley. The Romans conquering the land in 63 BCE took the name of the province of Judah to be the whole of the land.

The Talmud (a collection of Jewish, civil, and religious laws) in referring to Palestine speaks of it simply as "the land," a term that has endured in Jewish terminology to this day. The province basked in the great distinction of Jerusalem and the temple. The whole Diaspora looked upon it as the center of the world. Jerusalem's population estimated at 120,000 was at times swollen by masses of pilgrims, who periodically outnumbered the local population. The temple and the court provided permanent employment. Jerusalem was the seat of the high priest and the Sanhedrin, in which rich landowners, well-to-do merchants, and craftsmen found it attractive for settlement. There was a thriving business in luxuries, including precious stones and expensive cloth. But for the residents of Galilee, it was different. Their region was the main center of the common people. There were no great centers of learning and boasted no large cities or famous teachings. Its inhabitants could not compare in scholarship with the population that lived close to the splendor of the temple. Many dispossessed and landless could be found wandering from village to village. From these downtrodden Jews came Jesus of Nazareth.

> *The day following Jesus would go forth into Galilee, and findeth Philip, and saith unto him, Follow me. Now Philip was of Bethsaida, the city of Andrew and Peter. Philip findeth Nathanael, and saith unto him, We have found him, of whom Moses in the law, and the prophets, did write, Jesus of Nazareth, the son of Joseph. And Nathanael said unto him, Can there any good thing come out of Nazareth? Philip saith unto him, Come and see.*
> —John 1:43–46

Many agreed that if there ever was a time when they needed a deliverer in the likeness of Moses, it was then. However, things were different; they were already located in the land of promise, so they did not have to be physically drawn out of a particular place but rather drawn in spiritually and introduced to a whole new way of thinking, a new kingdom in which they would be regarded as prominent citizens—even as kings and princesses.

And when he was demanded of the Pharisees, when the kingdom of God should come, he answered them and said, The kingdom of God cometh not with observation: Neither shall they say, Lo here! or, lo there! for, behold, the kingdom of God is within you.

—Luke 17:20–21

This kind of language was offensive to some of the religious leaders of that era. They could not get their minds around or come to grips with the idea that a man who did not concur with their schools of thought, who had not set under the tutelage of the priesthood, would dare try and pass himself off as some new religious leader of the disenfranchised, both Jew and Gentile. And if that was not enough, this man Jesus also claimed to be "the Son of God."

Jesus answered them, Many good works have I shewed you from my Father; for which of those works do ye stone me? The Jews answered him, saying, For a good work we stone thee not; but for blasphemy; and because that thou, being a man, makest thy-

49

self God. Jesus answered them, Is it not written in your law, I said, Ye are gods? If he called them gods, unto whom the word of God came, and the scripture cannot be broken; Say ye of him, whom the Father hath sanctified, and sent into the world, Thou blasphemest; because I said, I am the Son of God?

—John 10:32–36

Obviously, even in the minds of those who sought after a deliverer, the prevailing question must have been, who could this person be, and where would He come from?

Undoubtedly, He would have to be a Jew because the Jews could never trust so great a task to anyone who was not of Jewish lineage.

And so, Matthew, in the New Testament, begins by tracing Jesus' bloodline forward through forty-two generations. However, this in and of itself would not be enough. The next daunting question would be, how could one mount this kind of a campaign without the support of the current religious leaders and their following? Or how could you build such a following when the Roman leaders were so quick to respond to that kind of activity?

In fact, a group calling itself the Zealots during that time became primary marks of aggression for trying to militarily oppose the Roman domination of Palestine and to incite a people's revolt against Roman tyranny and oppression. Because of the differences that existed between the religious sects of that day, i.e., Pharisees and Sadducees, there was little hope of any unified support from those who presided over the temple and the synagogues. Also, the multicultural demographics of the area posed another challenge. There were Jews, Greeks, Romans, and many other ethnic groups living in the region. What would be the single thread that would unite them and turn their hearts toward God and this love He so urgently wanted them to receive? God's answer to this dilemma was then and still is the enduring love of the Rose of Sharon.

I am the rose of Sharon, and the lily of the valleys.
—Song of Solomon 2:1

And leaving Nazareth, he came and dwelt in Capernaum, which is upon the sea coast, in the borders of Zabulon and Nephthalim: That it might be fulfilled which was spoken by Esaias the prophet, saying, The land of Zabulon, and the land of Nephthalim, by the way of the sea, beyond Jordan, Galilee of the Gentiles; the people which sat in darkness saw great light; and to them which sat in the region and shadow of death light is sprung up.
—Matthew 4:13–16

CHAPTER 6

A Call to Worship

But our God is in the heavens: he hath done what-soever he hath pleased. Their idols are silver and gold, the work of men's hands. They have mouths, but they speak not: eyes have they, but they see not: They have ears, but they hear not: noses have they, but they smell not: They have hands, but they han-dle not: feet have they, but they walk not: neither speak they through their throat. They that make them are like unto them; so is every one that trust-eth in them.

—Psalm 115:3–8

Let's talk about gods. We know all too well that there are other gods—gods made with men's hands that only lead them away from their true purpose. Throughout the Old Testament, we have been cautioned against them and those who promote them and their dead-end results: "[And] they that make them are [just] like unto them." Wherever they started out, that's where they end up.

That's why some people don't move, don't change; they generally keep the same things they have always had, attitudes, habits, downfalls, and suspicions. Whatever things they treasure or embrace don't grow spiritually. The gods (traditions) that they worship are dead.

Our God is a God of revelation, always presenting us with new ideas and approaches. Of course, they are not new to Him because they have always been around. But when we receive them, they are usually awesome by design and range. That's why the illumination that comes through foresight—"for he who hath an ear to hear"—will prevent us from being caught off guard.

> *Verily I say unto you, This generation shall not pass away, till all be fulfilled. Heaven and earth shall pass away: but my words shall not pass away. And take heed of yourselves, lest at any time your hearts be overcharged with surfeiting, and drunkenness, and cares of this life, and so that day come upon you unawares.*
>
> —Luke 21:32–34

> *But God hath revealed them unto us by his Spirit: for the Spirit searcheth all things, yea, the deep things of God. For what man knoweth the things of a man, save the spirit of man which is in him? even so the things of God knoweth no man, but the Spirit*

of God. Now we have received, not the spirit of the
world, but the spirit which is of God; that we might
know the things that are freely given to us of God.
—1 Corinthians 2:10–12

This God-given knowledge gives us the spiritual insight on how to best address certain inquiries and questions like, how can a loving God allow so many people to suffer the way that He does? That question can only be answered by those of us who understand God's plan of escape and have faith in that plan. The path of intimacy with God has always been through pain, suffering, and adversity. This is in no way an admittance of defeat, but it's our assurance by faith that we will always be victorious in Jesus. Also, with that being said, how can we know that God can perform unless there is first a need for His performance? It's this kind of reasoning that inspires us to cry out to Him. And in our doing so, it confirms that we know and believe that He will always be there.

This same cognitive thinking has the reverse effect on those who have not been introduced to the living God. Their hopes have been dashed, or they are left feeling unguarded or unprotected. These feelings are internalized, causing their senses to be dulled and their thinking to become mechanical. The only information they can process is that which comes through their natural senses, such as seeing, hearing, touching, and smelling. In other words, if they can't see or feel it, then it doesn't exist. This limits them in their ability to perceive or see beyond those things that challenge who they are.

For by him were all things created, that are in heaven, and that are in earth, visible and invisible, whether they be thrones, or dominions, or principalities, or powers: all things were created by him, and for him: And he is before all things, and by him all things consist.

—Colossians 1:16–17

This shows us once again that God is, in fact, a master planner. He is also a shaker and a mover. He is always shaking people up and moving them around. And it's during those times, more than ever, that we should try and strive not to lose our faith. Though circumstances are threatening to bury us, I have learned that sometimes God will allow us to appear to be sinking, just to prove that with Him, we can rise again.

And he said, LORD God, whereby shall I know that I shall inherit it?

—Genesis 15:8

So often, as is the case with God, His plan for Abraham went far beyond what the eyes or the mind of a man could foresee. Oftentimes God will call us to things that we just can't see. As the story goes, Abraham had a concern because God had made blood and blood ties a vital fact of life. Abraham was greatly disturbed over the fact that God had promised him great things, not only for himself, but for his seed and their seed after them.

The problem, at least in Abraham's mind, was that there were no heirs to receive and carry on after he was gone. He knew that he and his wife were much too old to conceive children of their own. God begins to dialogue with him and establish his faith through experience. Most often, we focus all our attention on the rough moments of the most trying events in our lives. It's a natural response to trouble, fear, doubt, or deep concern. As I have already stated, most of us can look back at those times when we were convinced there was no solution to our problem. This was, in fact, the big one, but lo and behold, the blood prevailed, and we got out. And it's all because the love of God persisted that we were able to mount up with eagle's wings, soar above it all, and survive.

After taking God's response to our issues into account, we must be open to other gateways other than our natural senses. This is what God reminded Abraham of, that He had called him out from an unbelieving people who were worshiping idol gods. Abraham's human skepticism had kicked in. Though God does not want us to rely on human feelings when it comes to His promises, He will indulge us. God's response to Abraham's question, *"...whereby shall I know that I shall inherit it?"* (Genesis 15:8) was to request a sacrifice.

And he said unto him, Take me an heifer of three years old, and a she goat of three years old, and a ram of three years old, and a turtledove, and a young pigeon.
—Genesis 15:9

In other words, "Turn all your attention toward Me and what I have instructed you to do, and I will richly bless you." If you are earnestly coming before God, you should not do so without bringing with you something that has substance and value. Part of our obligation to serve is to step out by faith onto unparted waters. Let me state emphatically that there is an enormous difference between celebrating God and serving Him. To celebrate God is to elevate, amplify, and magnify Him. To serve Him is to be willing to roll up our sleeves, reach out, and touch someone else's pain. Such as with our brothers and sisters who are holding fast to their faith in underground churches.

There are just too many of us who want to be without becoming. God is looking for that humble doer that is willing to serve without seeking vainglory. Bring Him something—your mind, your heart, or a willingness to support a work of His that is taking place in the earth.

This might also include a word of truth that has been imparted to you to share with others. The Bible calls it being workers together with God, an interaction whose part is to create a fire in us by way of His Holy Spirit. This union teaches us to walk in faith and favor and to cooperate with God. He operates in favor when we operate in faith. Abraham felt as though he belonged because God gave him the opportunity to cooperate (to operate in union with another).

The moment that Abraham laid out his offering, the Scripture tells us the fowls came down upon the carcasses and Abraham drove them away. Abraham had decided that although they were ignorant to what was going on between him and God, as many are, he had to separate himself from them. There are some who will oppose us and not even know why, simply because tradition says they should. In Abraham's case, the actions of the fowl were in direct opposition to what God and Abraham had agreed upon. He, therefore, decided to protect that which he had covenanted to offer up to God. God could have intervened, but He didn't; it was Abraham's job to stand in defense of that which he knew was his.

When it comes to establishing and keeping covenant with God, there are some things we cannot do, like breaking through walls of dissension. Wisdom dictates that we leave those things up to Him, knowing full well that in His own time and in His own way, He will do them. However, no matter how He (God) might choose to move, our hearts must still be directed toward Him, knowing that what may appear to be a delay or denial on God's part is, in fact, a call to worship, which is something that we certainly can do.

Faith is an action word because believing is something that God expects to be done. What if Abraham had decided there was no need to continue with his sacrifice because the buzzards were going to get it anyway, because trouble was going to come against it, because challenges were going to rise? What would he have accomplished with an attitude of defeat? Absolutely nothing. It is a known fact that opposition will be lurking around somewhere, looking for a favorable opportunity to attack and try to force us to abort our mission. But those chosen are no strangers to distress, anguish, and travail.

> *And he said unto Abram, Know of a surety that thy seed shall be a stranger in a land that is not theirs, and shall serve them; and they shall afflict them four hundred years; And also that nation, whom they shall serve, will I judge: and afterward shall they come out with great substance.*
>
> —Genesis 15:13–14

Here in Genesis, God forewarns Abraham of a time when his seed would go into Egyptian captivity. He also assures him that after four hundred years, He would judge that nation that persecuted them. When the time for their deliverance came, the Hebrews would emerge from that captivity with great substance. This is how God explained it to Moses:

> *And the LORD said, I have surely seen the affliction of my people which are in Egypt, and have heard their cry by reason of their taskmasters; for I know their sorrows; and I am come down to deliver them out of the hand of the Egyptians, and to bring them up out of that land unto a good land and a large, unto a land flowing with milk and honey; unto the place of the Canaanites, and the Hittites, and the Amorites, and the Perizzites, and the Hivites, and the Jebusites.*
>
> —Exodus 3:7–8

God's desire for worship had been consummated. Israel's cries unto Him caused Jehovah Shalom (the Lord of peace) to move into action on their behalf. Israel's deliverance is not a chronicle of their being rescued by hordes of outside sword-swinging, superhuman warriors. It does not resemble the reckless abandon of a heroic world, such as the Greeks, Muslims, and other ancient people saw as their original state.

Stories of Abraham, Isaac, Jacob, Joseph, and even Moses are permeated by a sense of divine destiny. They also contain a much simpler, God-like law and tradition. A tradition that dismisses the recognizable way of human life in which combat and cunning prevail and replaces it with gentler affections of a close-knit family. In each instance throughout the generations, God's chosen were always immersed in His spoken word. That word acted as a kind of anchor when all around them seemed to be moving in multiple directions. It is extremely notable that those same words that directed the lives of the patriarchs and trailblazers who have gone on before us will be as loud and pertinent today as they ever were.

What I tell you in darkness, that speak ye in light: and what ye hear in the ear, that preach ye upon the housetops.
—Matthew 10:27

This could only be seen as a prophetic dispersion that is as accurate and forceful as when it was first spoken. The emergence of this faith has always been accurately described as a revolution in the world's view of man. All previous and contemporary religions saw human destiny as subject to the laws of nature. Just as the natural cycles returned to their point of origin having no real purpose, so was human life conceived as an endless possession passing through birth and chaos, eventually ending once again in the same darkness and chaos from which it came.

The gods themselves were subject to human passion, incest, and lust. They were associated with natural origins and energies, such as sun, light, air, and fertility. Natural forces were numerous, and so were these gods. There was a god for each force at the point of chaos.

The Jew and the Christian, however, always received a sense of belonging or nurturing that is unprecedented or unmatched throughout history. This knowledge is essential in our quest to occupy and make our presence known until our Lord returns. Therefore, for us, there is no turning but rather this delightful, enchanting possibility of our being able to return again. As a result of frustration, intimidation, and despair, many a pilgrim have turned and walked away, abandoning the faith, leaving in its place a pile of rubble made up of dreams, ideas, and promises that may never be realized.

Even now, many remain preoccupied with the question as to why God would allow evil to exist. The first thing we must understand is that with God, every round goes higher. Earlier in this book, we have had the opportunity to look at this huge canvas upon which God has not yet completed His masterpiece. If you ever decorate a Christmas tree or watch someone else do so, you will notice that with all the beautiful ornaments, all the beautiful lights, it's still not complete until it is crowned with the star. God is building something that is eternal in nature, and we are all part of that work in progress. We must learn to see a bigger picture, a picture of which you and I have a part, a picture much bigger than anything that we will have to face in this world. It's not about suffering. It's not even about living or dying; it's all about divine design. Any part of us that we exercise the most will become the strongest part.

Therefore, those individuals who exercise fear, hatred, racial prejudice, oppression, betrayal, and vile affection will become strong in those areas. But we are told to exercise our faith through praise, prayer, worship, and love. The apostle Paul was a shining example of this.

> *I have planted, Apollos watered; but God gave the increase.*
> —1 Corinthians 3:6

Both Paul and Apollos became living sacrifices unto God in that they had given their entire lives for the work of the ministry. As a result of their sacrifice, God gave them increase. No matter what one might be going through or how bad things may appear to be, we must remember that it's only a prelude to greater things, and if we continue to trust and worship God, there's only one way we can go, and that is over and above, higher into heavenly places.

But what things were gain to me, those I counted loss for Christ. Yea doubtless, and I count all things but loss for the excellently of the knowledge of Christ Jesus my Lord: for whom I have suffered the loss of all things, and do count them but dung, that I may win Christ.

—Philippians 3:7–8

Paul was an adventurer who knew God in a way that most men had not known Him, and for this reason, he would not allow himself to be hemmed in by traditions established by men, even those of his own company. Paul was concerned that the Church would find herself going around in circles instead of forging ahead toward the greatness that was assigned to her. Paul understood that through the blood of Christ, by faith, he was tied to something that was bigger than life itself. He refused to let anyone make little of that fact. Just listen to this statement with your heart, considering some of the things I have already shared with you.

For we know that the whole creation groaneth and travaileth in pain together until now. And not only they, but ourselves also, which have the firstfruits of the Spirit, even we ourselves

groan within ourselves, waiting for the adoption, to wit, the re-
demption of our body.

—Romans 8:22–23

Here, the creature is groaning deep within itself to become one once again with all of creation. Paul calls it the adoption of the sons of God, both Jew and Gentile, being grafted into the universal family, and this, without a doubt, will be a crowning moment.

Beloved, now are we the sons of God, and it doth not yet ap-
pear what we shall be: but we know that, when he shall appear,
we shall be like him; for we shall see him as he is.

—1 John 3:2

If you are a believer, this should surely stir your imagination and cause you to wonder what this moment could be like.

Be merciful unto me, O God, be merciful unto me: for my
soul trusteth in thee: yea, in the shadow of thy wings will I
make my refuge, until these calamities be overpast. I will cry
unto God most high; unto God that peformeth all things for me.

—Psalm 57:1–2

This psalm and all that it encompasses certainly shed light on the hymn that says, *"Amazing grace how sweet the sound; that saved a wretch like me. I once was lost, but now I'm found; was blind, but now I see."*[1]

What a wonderful blessing it is when God allows us to be able to see beyond the trials of our natural surroundings and be able to call on Him from those places of despair, allowing us to understand His motives and share with others His magnificent plan of salvation, a plan that includes the coming together of both Jews and Gentiles in His Church. As we answer this exciting *call to worship*, it gives rise to our being able to begin again, with the eyes of the Lord leading the way through visions and dreams, for this is truly the next level of progression for this select group who are identified in Scripture as those *"sons and daughters, who in these last days, will prophesy"* (Joel 2:28).

---

1 Hugh Wilson, *The National Baptist Hymnal*, p. 135.

CHAPTER 7

The Twain Becoming One

For he is our peace, who hath made both one, and hath broken down the middle wall of partition between us; having abolished in his flesh the enmity, even the law of commandments contained in ordinances; for to make in himself of twain one new man, so making peace.

—Ephesians 2:14–15

By the rivers of Babylon, there we sat down, yea, we wept, when we remembered Zion. We hanged our harps upon the willows in the midst thereof. For there they that carried us away captive required of us a song; and they that wasted us required of us mirth, saying, Sing us one of the songs of Zion. How shall we sing the LORD's song in a strange land? If I forget thee, O Jerusalem, let my right hand forget her cunning. If I do not remember thee, let my

*tongue cleave to the roof of my mouth; if I prefer not
Jerusalem above my chief joy.*

—Psalm 137:1–6

*But ye are a chosen generation, a royal priesthood,
an holy nation, a peculiar people; that ye should
shew forth the praises of him who hath called you
out of darkness into his marvellous light: Which in
time past were not a people, but are now the people
of God: which had not obtained mercy, but now
have obtained mercy.*

—1 Peter 2:9–10

In both these literary movements, there is an air of
poetic splendor, grace, and acceptance. The resolve that
emanates from these voices of the past speaks directly
to the heart of all that is loved, shared, and reverenced
by an ensemble of people who openly acknowledge the
favor of God upon their lives. One is by divine birth-
right; the other has been grafted in according to the
election of grace. *Israel, the chosen people,* is lamenting
as though a huge door had been slammed shut against
them, separating them from their divine heritage. *"How
shall we sing the songs of Zion in a strange land?"* (see Psalm
137:4). And the Church, the chosen generation, who believed that a huge door had been opened to them as a
direct result of this decidedly new covenant twist that

was initiated by Jesus on Calvary... *"a people who were not a people, but who have now become the people of God"* (see 1 Peter 2:10).

Both these groups collectively make up a select remnant of believers that God is assembling at this crucial juncture of the Judeo-Christian legacy. It all began to change in 1948, when Israel's door to God's promises was reopened. She was widely accepted by much of the world as a sovereign nation. For the Jews, this was a moment that was way overdue. A moment that they felt had been purchased by the blood, sweat, and tears of millions of their fellow laborers. For the Church, they understood that their deliverance had all been purchased by the blood, sweat, and tears of our Lord Jesus Christ. From this agonizing reminiscence, a phrase was infused to symbolize a well-deserved independence of a determined people. The phrase affectionately embraced was *"never again."*

> *So shall my word be that goeth forth out of my mouth: it shall not return unto me void, but it shall accomplish that which I please, and it shall prosper in the thing whereto I sent it. For ye shall go out with joy, and be led forth with peace: the mountains and the hills shall break forth before you into singing, and all the trees of the field shall clap their hands. Instead of the thorn shall come up the fir tree, and*

instead of the brier shall come up the myrtle tree:
and it shall be to the LORD for a name, for an ever-
lasting sign that shall not be cut off.

—Isaiah 55:11–13

Immediately after the formation of what was called the State of Israel, the Jewish people began to reach out in all directions for their oppressed brothers and sisters, those who had been exiled from their homeland for far too long. *At the same time, the Spirit of the Lord was rapidly moving across the globe, as the Word of God was being preached to every nation, kindred, and tongue.* All in accordance with the instructions Jesus left with His disciples, who were then able to pass them on to every Christian generation that would succeed them.

Go ye therefore, and teach all nations, baptizing them in the name of the Father, and of the Son, and of the Holy Ghost: Teaching them to observe all things whatsoever I have commanded you: and, lo, I am with you always, even unto the end of the world. Amen.

—Matthew 28:19–20

Unbeknownst to many, Gods' end-time plan was in full swing and, as always, right on schedule. All the way up to our individual conversions, yours and mine.

But blessed are your eyes, for they see: and your ears, for they hear.

—Matthew 13:16

In the winters of 1948 and 1949, the camps in Cyprus where the British had held thousands of Jews were finally closed. Israeli forces seized an Egyptian stronghold in Beersheba, later Galilee, and old communities of Yemen and Iraq where Jews had lived before Muslim and Arab history had begun. The creation of a Jewish state was like the sound of a trumpet, calling them to change the direction of their lives and to join the construction of a new society, one which was preordained before any of these things ever came into play.

Blow ye the trumped in Zion, and sound an alarm in my holy mountain: let all the inhabitants of the land tremble: for the day of the LORD cometh, for it is nigh at hand.

—Joel 2:1

Most of the world was shocked at the speed and efficacy in which Israel was able to move.

Who hath heard such a thing? who hath seen such things? Shall the earth be made to bring forth in one day? or shall a nation be born at once? for as soon as Zion travailed, she brought forth her children.

—Isaiah 66:8

Operation Magic Carpet lifted thousands of Midianite Jews to Israel, the last of them in September 1950. As with most sovereign countries, there are three main factors that constitute the staples of commitment to the people of that nation: security, economics, and progress. To date, Israel's military is one of the most formidable in the modern world. Its army, air force, and navy are all well-manned and ready to move at a moment's notice.

After 1956, the next ten years proved to be the most fertile progression in Israel's history. Israel prospered, the economy flourished, immigration had increased, and her international position had broadened year by year. Ninety-one Israeli embassies existed in all the five continents of the world. None of these accomplishments, however, came without great cost. The Jews paid dearly for every inch of ground they recovered. That's why to ensure continued progress, Israel's leaders must use sound judgment in determining who their real allies are. The twain becoming one would enable them to recognize essential strategies that should be set in motion for the greater good.

A new commandment I give unto you, that ye love one another; as I have loved you, that ye also love one another. By this shall all men know that ye are my disciples, if ye have love one to another.

—John 13:34–35

This would require a sincere collaboration with some who presently might exist outside of her normal, social, or religious parameters. Of course, before such an arrangement could be taken seriously, there would first have to be a considerable amount of trust. Trust is a strong reliance, confidence, and belief that is formulated when one party or group is convinced that others understand their hopes, dreams, ideas, concerns, and values. They will never violate them. Mutual trust is when the other party believes that they can expect the same thing in return. As far as having something in common is concerned, for the most part, both Jew and Christian have been persecuted and are now being threatened by the same enemies.

> *And who is he that will harm you, if ye be followers of that which is good? But and if ye suffer for righteousness' sake, happy are ye: and be not afraid of their terror, neither be troubled; but sanctify the Lord God in your hearts: and be ready always to give an answer to every man that asketh you a reason of the hope that is in you with meekness and fear.*
> —1 Peter 3:13–15

This epistle was written by a Jewish brother who was operating under a dangerous set of circumstances. He was trying to promote an unpopular doctrine. Many of his company had already been placed in prison or worst. Yet under heavy persecution, he still found it within himself to encourage or remind those who remained true to their convictions that because they were on the side of good, they should not be afraid. Therefore, he wrote, "Be ready always to give an answer to every man that asks you a reason for the hope that is within you. Not in a brazen high-minded kind of way but in meekness and fear." These prophetic answers will come from those whose lips have been scorched with a decisive word, one that adds credence to all God has done, is doing, and will ultimately bring to pass.

> *Then said I, Woe is me! for I am undone; because I am a man of unclean lips, and I dwell in the midst of a people of unclean lips: for mine eyes have seen the King, the LORD of hosts. Then flew one of the seraphims unto me, having a live coal in his hand, which he had taken with the tongs from off the altar: And he laid it upon my mouth, and said, Lo, this hath touched thy lips; and thine iniquity is taken away, and thy sin purged. Also I heard the voice of the Lord, saying, Whom shall I send, and who will go for us? Then said I, Here am I; send me.*
> —Isaiah 6:5–8

We understand the uncompromising need for the twain to become one; that's why we are called "infidels" by those who have sworn to destroy us both. At least in that regard, and in the interest of taking action for the greater good, it is essential that we unite our efforts against those who are rapidly mounting their efforts against us. Our assignment is to step out on that which we know to be right, to submerge ourselves into the things that we preach because the action of the witness is more compelling than the words that proceed out of their mouths. As a chosen generation, our primary goal is to set an agenda that is based on the reconciled Word of God.

> *And all things are of God, who hath reconciled us to himself by Jesus Christ, and hath given to us the ministry of reconciliation; to wit, that God was in Christ, reconciling the world unto himself, not imputing their trespasses unto them; and hath committed unto us the word of reconciliation.*
> —2 Corinthians 5:18–19

This passage substantiates our assertion that Israel's (the church's) history is God's gift to the world. "They shall prosper that love thee" (Psalm 122:6). God has set in place a directive that will foster dialogue culminating in tremendous blessings for those who love both Israel and the Church. This is not just an opportunity that God is offering a few enlightened people; this is a mandate for the entire body of Christ. It is imperative for the greater good of Israel and the Church that both Jew and Gentile Christians learn to trust each other. As we move forward, we must be willing to tackle head-on those things that might abate our progress or confuse our primary objective. For the greater good of this select body, we must pray for wisdom and honesty within our ranks, knowing that our first challenge will be finding ways to confront the prejudices and suspicions that are mostly born out of tradition and maintained by a sense of loyalty to those who have passed them on to us.

Now I beseech you, brethren, by the name of our Lord Jesus Christ, that ye all speak the same thing, and that there be no divisions among you; but that ye be perfectly joined together in the same mind and in the same judgment.

—1 Corinthians 1:10

Here, the writer, Paul, is dealing with what I'm going to term "learned behavior." He has a group of people from diverse backgrounds who have different opinions, attitudes, and ideas about how a certain thing should be approached. So as not to appear intrusive or to belittle their way of reasoning, he begins by saying, "I employ you, brethren, in the name of Him whom we all trust and for the sake of the greater good that we seek common ground."

In the standard of awareness, again, we find this encouraging reference to a single-minded prophetic word from God.

> *I was in the city of Joppa praying: and in a trance I saw a vision, a certain vessel descend, as it had been a great sheet, let down from heaven by four corners; and it came even to me: Upon the which when I had fastened mine eyes, I considered, and saw fourfooted beasts of the earth, and wild beasts, and creeping things, and fowls of the air. And I heard a voice saying unto me, Peter; slay and eat. But I said, Not so, Lord: for nothing common or unclean hath at any time entered into my mouth. But the voice answered me again from heaven, What God hath cleansed, that call not thou common.*
>
> —Acts 11:5–9

Through a vision, the apostle Peter was given a contentious change of direction, inferring or concluding that from that point forward, Gentiles would be accepted into the body of believers, and both Jew and Gentile could and would become one in Christ.

> *For, brethren, ye have been called into liberty; only use not liberty for an occasion to the flesh, but by love serve one anoth-*

er. For all of the law is fulfilled in one word, even in this; Thou shalt love thy neighbour as thyself.

—Galatians 5:13–14

In this text, we can see how the apostle Paul is called to display the heart of God to the Gentiles. He is addressing people who knew all too well what it was like to live under tyranny, shame, and oppression. His inference here is that too often, those who have been set free from physical, emotional, or mental imprisonment will tend to want to celebrate.

The problem is that the only example of celebration was that which they had learned by observing their former captors. It's never a good idea to try and imitate those who might see you as not being equal. Paul informs them that they had been "called to liberty." This meant that their freedom did not come because of a change of heart of their oppressors but because of a supernatural decree from an unseen power.

This is a force greater than anyone could challenge or even fully comprehend, He whom we worship, God. Paul informs us that there is no room for vainglory or selfish intent. We must learn to channel our enthusiasm through the corridors of *love* with a commitment to serve. It's in that same spirit that we must present ourselves to our beloved companion Israel. To build her confidence that as the Church, we not only applauded this magnificent union, but we are also determined to accept the irrevocable truth that for us to take full guardianship of every benefit afforded to us by Christ and His amazing work on that cross; *the twain must become one.*

CHAPTER 8

The Intrusion of the Strongman

No man can enter into a strong man's house, and spoil his goods, except he will first bind the strong man; and then he will spoil his house.

—Mark 3:27

As you may know, the strongman Jesus is referring to is Satan, the adversary. An outsider who had managed, through violent assault, to enter, lay siege upon, and take possession of another's house or property. For the rightful owner to recover their goods, they must first uncover a way to bind that strongman. Of course, the only way to do that is to enlist the services or employ the actions of a stronger man. Hence, one that is totally augmented by the power of God's presence.

For the eyes of the LORD run to and fro throughout the whole earth, to shew himself strong in the behalf of them whose heart is perfect toward him. Herein thou hast done foolishly: therefore from henceforth thou shalt have wars.

—2 Chronicles 16:9

And ye shall seek me, and find me, when ye shall search for me with all your heart.

—Jeremiah 29:13

For those who were inclined to hear and respond to the spiritual insight His prophets were offering, God would consistently afford them a glimpse into future events *"...from henceforth thou shall have wars"* (2 Chronicles 16:9). What both these writers, Solomon the king and Jeremiah the prophet, are advocating is that one sincere heartfelt outpouring to God can be more successful at binding the strongman than an entire army fully arrayed for battle.

In His resolve to steer His Church toward one Lord, one faith, and one baptism, it seems that the Israelites, like so many other chosen of God, had never experienced any length of time when they did not have to deal with the advances of the strongman and his agents, each seeing himself as a strongman. All these antagonists were determined to deny the well-being of God's Church.

But through it all, whenever the time was right, by way of a prophetic discourse, God never ceased to bolster their walk of faith as they endeavored to keep cadence on an uncharted journey toward a divine legacy.

Behold, the former things are come to pass, and new things do I declare: before they spring forth I tell you of them.
—Isaiah 42:9

This is a story that would be repeated over and over again.

For the vision is yet for an appointed time, but at the end it shall speak, and not lie: though it tarry, wait for it; because it will surely come, it will not tarry.
—Habakkuk 2:3

In the end, it shall speak and not lie. What appears to be an endless drawn-out marathon for us is only a very small sprint for God.

There was a span of two hundred years between the conquering of Babylon by Cyrus the Great of Persia, a strongman; the re-founding of the Jewish nation under the leadership of Nehemiah and Ezra; and the destruction of the Persian Empire by Alexander the Great, another strongman. Alexander was a young Greek general who defeated the Persian Emperor Darius III at a place called Issus. Physically speaking, all these men and the armies that they commanded were huge and very strong, but God was constantly penetrating their ranks.

All the kings of the earth shall praise thee, O LORD, when they hear the words of thy mouth.

—Psalm 138:4

These words always have and always will come from the mouths of those endowed with the gift of prophecy, those carrying a well-timed opportune word.

Wherefore I also, after I heard of your faith in the Lord Jesus, and love unto all the saints, cease not to give thanks for you, making mention of you in my prayers; that the God of our Lord Jesus Christ, the Father of glory, may give unto you the spirit of wisdom and revelation in the knowledge of him: The eyes of your understanding being enlightened; that ye may know what is the hope of his calling, and what the riches of the glory of his inheritance in the saints, and what is the exceeding greatness of his power to us-ward who believe, according to the working of his mighty power.

—Ephesians 1:15–19

Just listen to the apostle Paul in writing to those that believe and have a fervent love for the church. From the depths of his soul, he's praying and calling out to God *"...that ye may know what is the hope of his calling..."* (verse

18), and that by the gift of God's spirit of wisdom and revelation, you will have the power to stand against the strongman, no matter what form he may take or as whom he might present himself to you.

Paul says that because you are now a seer, "...*The eyes of your understanding being enlightened...*" (verse 18), you have been made to sit together in heavenly places with Christ Jesus, and by a divine entrance into the lives of others, it has been entrusted to you to stand guard over God's rich inheritance in the saints.

The great empire created by Alexander to date has never been rivaled. It has been noted that his army of Macedonian and Greek troops numbered close to thirty thousand foot soldiers and five thousand cavalry. All these well-trained, well-equipped, strongmen were able to overthrow the highly fragmented and unorganized Persian Empire within a four-year period. Alexander's campaign surged without any credible resistance. It spanned from Asia Minor to Egypt, from Egypt to Central Asia, and then to the Indus Valley in India. Wherever he went, Alexander founded or re-founded Greek-style cities with his own name, spreading Hellenistic (Greek) city-based culture over the whole empire.

By 332 BCE, Alexander, the strongman, conquered Judea. As a result, the influence of Hellenism on the Jews increased. The strong arm of the strongman was in place, acting as a vise to hold and secure the furtherance of the Greek culture into the lives and subsistence of the Jewish people. In fact, it soon became necessary if one wanted to be successful to obtain a Greek education. Many Jews accepted this intrusion of the strongman readily. They often welcomed those Jews who spoke Greek and had adopted Greek culture to the temple when they returned from pilgrimage.

For the conservative Jews, however, this whole Hellenistic (Greek) idea was not a good one. They hated the Greek customs and influences on their people. Activities, such as wrestling and athletics, were highly detested. For this reason, some refused to be intimidated by the antics of the strongman, as they rehearsed among themselves the anthems of praise sung by Moses and the people of Israel after they were delivered from the clutches of Pharaoh and the Egyptians.

The LORD is my strength and song, and he is become my salvation: he is my God, and I will prepare him an habitation; my father's God, and I will exalt him. The LORD is a man of war: The LORD is his name.

—Exodus 15:2–3

The clear challenge facing the Jewish nation at that time was how a psychologically conquered people could combat the aggression and intrusions of the strongman. I say psychologically conquered because even to this very day, Israel's enemies still fear their God. The question to be answered by Israel's enemies then and now is, how do we keep this remnant from joining ranks with others of like spirits and calling on their God with one voice?

Submit yourselves therefore to God. Resist the devil, and he will flee from you.

—James 4:7

This Scripture was written by the apostle James, the last man standing on behalf of the original Christian alliance between Jew and Gentile. The operative words here are "submit" and "resist." Here is how the apostle Paul addresses this same question of how to rebound from the intrusion of the strongman:

Finally, my brethren, be strong in the Lord, and in the power of his might.

—Ephesians 6:10

Both the apostles James and Paul are talking about a surrender of a different sort, not into the hands of the strongman but rather a yielding or a relinquishing of our plans and programs over to the plan that God has prearranged to publicly express a willingness to take part in the promotion of this predetermined, providential idea. One that had proven itself to produce an even stronger counterattack against the strongman.

So shall they fear the name of the LORD from the west, and his glory from the rising of the sun. When the enemy shall come in like a flood, the Spirit of the LORD shall lift up a standard against him.

—Isaiah 59:19

As a result of Israel's desperate need for revival at that time, a variety of religious groups emerged within Judaism. Two of these groups were the Pharisees and Sadducees. Although they differed on their approach in some areas to the Jewish religion, they both held a disdain for the Greek or Hellenistic mythologies and ideals. The Pharisees insisted on the strict observance of Jewish ritual laws. They demanded that those of their groups obey the rules of food and purity. They also isolated themselves from non-Pharisees. These men were very influential in the Jews' supreme court and legislative body, the Sanhedrin.

The Sadducees, on the other hand, had exercised considerable political and spiritual influence. Most of them were wealthy, and included among their group were the high priest and president of the Sanhedrin. Both groups understood, however, the need for resistance. They knew religious tolerance should not be confused with religious freedom. And so, they recognized their situation for what it was, religious tolerance. In other words, they were allowed to have beliefs but were certainly not allowed to exercise those things they believed in, to the fullest extent.

After the death of Alexander the Great in 323 BC, a Greek general by the name of Antiochus, another strongman, launched an attack on the Jewish religion in 170 BC. He longed for the wealth of the temple in Jerusalem. Antiochus sent in troops to put down unrest and resistance. These troops looted the city and pulled down its walls, but they didn't destroy the temple. However, by 70 AD, Titus, the son of the Roman Emperor Vespasian, another strongman, laid siege to Jerusalem with an army of four legions. Having breached the walls, Roman troops stormed the temple, and by September of that year, the temple with all its splendor and treasure was looted and destroyed.

And as some spake of the temple, how it was adorned with goodly stones and gifts, he said, As for these things which ye behold, the days will come, in the which there shall not be left one stone upon another, that shall not be thrown down.

—Luke 21:5–6

One can only imagine how often these undervalued, disregarded people had to remind themselves and those of their bloodlines that no word from God would ever fail. One strongman after another seemed bent on robbing the Jews of their destiny as sole heirs of this undersized piece of real estate that caps the African continent.

In assessing the extraordinary value that the world powers have assigned to its strategic location, I submit that she, Israel, through the efforts of the Renascent Church, should one day be recognized as the crown of Africa. What an encouraging thought considering the current state of Africa today. One thing is certain, no matter how overriding and resistant the strongman may appear, he can and will be defeated and humbled by that which God has set in place.

> And there were certain Greeks among them that came up to worship at the feast: The same came therefore to Philip, which was of Bethsaida of Galilee, and desired him, saying, Sir, we would see Jesus. Philip cometh and telleth Andrew: and again Andrew and Philip tell Jesus. And Jesus answered them, saying, The hour is come, that the Son of man should be glorified.
>
> —John 12:20–23

CHAPTER 9

An Engaging Destiny

*For I would not, brethren, that ye should be igno-
rant of this mystery, lest ye should be wise in your
own conceits; that blindness in part is happened
to Israel, until the fulness of the Gentiles be come
in. And so all Israel shall be saved: as it is written,
There shall come out of Sion the Deliverer, and shall
turn away ungodliness from Jacob: For this is my
covenant unto them, when I shall take away their
sins.*

—Romans 11:25–27

Here in the book of Romans, the apostle Paul is
speaking of an event that he foresaw taking place in the
then distant future. *"...until the fulness of the Gentiles be
come in."* In this present age, Gentiles are co-equal with
Israel in terms of receiving their spiritual blessings
from God in the Church. The fulness of the Gentiles will

be completed when God's present task of winning Jew and Gentile to Christ is finalized. We know, however, that in order for these things to take place, it's going to take a concise word from God Himself, ushering in a prophetic certainty from the mouths of those He has summoned for the mission.

Till we all come in the unity of the faith, and of the knowledge of the Son of God, unto a perfect man, unto the measure of the stature of the fulness of Christ.
—Ephesians 4:13

His foundation is in the holy mountains. The LORD loveth the gates of Zion more than all the dwellings of Jacob. Glorious things are spoken of thee, O city of God. Selah.
—Psalm 87:1–3

The term engaging is defined as "winning, enchanting, captivating, disarming, and lovable." That's why this short psalm classified as a Song of Zion is one of the most engaging in the entire collection of Psalm. On the one hand, it is remarkably brief and to the point, almost to the place of being hidden or unnoticed. While on the other, its deep-seated love for Jerusalem is so passionately expressed when a Hebrew finds his foundation, his purpose, his entire being couched or entrenched in the holy mountains. The gates and the marketplaces are the center of the economic and social life of Jerusalem. Here in Scripture, the gates also represent the whole city, a city that God loves even more than the dwelling places of Jacob, which is any place where Israelis reside.

The glorious things that the psalmist may have had in mind are:

a. "The LORD hath chosen Zion . . . for his habitation" (Psalm 132:13).
b. "The mountain of his holiness, beautiful for situation, the joy of the whole earth" (Psalm 48:1–2).
c. Isaiah 2:3:

And many people shall go and say, Come ye, and let us go up to the mountain of the LORD, to the house of the God of Jacob; and he will teach us of his ways, and we will walk in his paths: for out of Zion shall go forth the law, and the word of the LORD from Jerusalem.

Notice how Jesus relays this same objective to the New Testament believer.

Ye are the light of the world. A city that is set on an hill cannot be hid.

—Matthew 5:14

In Psalm 87, the prophet of God had seen through prophetic lenses the global influence of God's chosen on future events.

All these glorious things are spoken of the city of God. The first and most obvious glory of the city is geographical. It was built on a mountainous pedestal from which it dominated the world and to which it drew the eyes of the nations of the earth. Small wonder why in the book of Matthew, as stated above, Jesus makes this marvelous correlation between ancient Israel and the present-day Church.

> *By faith Abraham, when he was called to go out into a place which he should after receive for an inheritance, obeyed; and he went out, not knowing whither he went. By faith he sojourned in the land of promise, as in a strange country, dwelling in tabernacles with Isaac and Jacob, the heirs with him of the same promise: For he looked for a city which hath foundations, whose builder and maker is God.*
> —Hebrews 11:8–10

> *Now therefore ye are no more strangers and foreigners, but fellowcitizens with the saints, and of the household of God; And are built upon the foundation of the apostles and prophets, Jesus Christ himself being the chief corner stone.*
> —Ephesians 2:19–20

These were the engaging things spoken both about Zion and the church, and glorious indeed they were. Just as with the definition of "increase," "to build upon" is "to expand or elevate to a greater degree," and once again, that includes the office of prophecy. It is hard to imagine one having these phenomenal deep-seated ties to their place in God and it not being reflected in their lives on a regular basis.

These things have I spoken unto you in proverbs: but the time cometh, when I shall no more speak unto you in proverbs, but I shall shew you plainly of the Father.

—John 16:25

What a startling revelation for those whose souls can now make their boast in the Lord that all their directives will come straight from the throne room. Now, I can't speak for anyone else, but I am so loving how these consistent testimonials, both in the Old and New Testaments, clearly show that from Genesis to Jesus, we, the *modern-day Renascent Church*, were always there.

Out of humble beginnings is greatness spawned; I don't know if anyone has ever made this assertion before, but it sounded good to me, and so I've said it.

Just as a matter of observation, Israel's destiny seems to have had a mind all its own. Even when the people didn't know who they were or where they were headed, prosperity followed them wherever they went. Much as with the origins of the Church.

The people which sat in darkness saw great light; and to them which sat in the region and shadow of death light is sprung up.
—Matthew 4:16

And they, continuing daily with one accord in the temple, and breaking bread from house to house, did eat their meat with gladness and singleness of heart, praising God, and having favour with all the people. And the Lord added to the church daily such as should be saved.
—Acts 2:46–47

When Israel entered Canaan, she was not a nation. Her formative years still lay ahead of her. The transitions from a semi-migratory or wandering people to an agricultural society, the transformation from tribe to nation were all influenced by contact with the populations of Canaan.

There must have been periods of peaceful relations among the Israelites and Canaanites because we know that a merging of cultures took place. The Israelites settled among a civilization higher than their own. But it was as though this mysterious ambiance surrounded them and directed their every move.

Fear thou not; for I am with thee: be not dismayed; for I am thy God: I will strengthen thee; yea, I will help thee; yea, I will uphold thee with the right hand of my righteousness.

—Isaiah 41:10

The material condition of the Israelites slowly improved. They became a nation of small farmers. They learned to build artificial reservoirs and underground tanks for storing water for use during dry seasons. In dire need of more soil, they showed resourcefulness and reclaimed land from deserts and forests. Their towns, few and badly fortified, were more of the pasture or rural nature, unlike the strongholds of the Canaanites and Philistines. Israel's strength depended on the number of men under arms who could be mustered in case of need and this unseen wall of protection that their God had placed around them. Often, tribal law was perceived to have prevailed against Israel's larger or greater interest.

In those days there was no king in Israel, but every man did that which was right in his own eyes.

—Judges 17:6

Two centuries (1230 BC–1030 BC) divide the conquest of Canaan from the reign of Israel's first king,

Saul. There were no political groups or heads of state to issue directives on how the country should be governed or what direction it should take. These were known as the days when judges ruled. In times of crisis, the people would make their appeal to the judges (gates, if you will), who were the overseers of the public's interest.

Even before the judges, Abraham and his nephew Lot showed examples of inner tribal conflict. They were all of one clan but had different herdsmen who disputed over land and water rights. Abraham, desiring to put an end to the discord, gave Lot the right of first choice.

Then Lot chose him all the plain of Jordan; and Lot journeyed east: and they separated themselves the one from the other. Abram dwelled in the land of Canaan, and Lot dwelled in the cities of the plain, and pitched his tent toward Sodom.

—Genesis 13:11–12

Because of the loss of Lot, Abraham feared even more that God could not keep His promises concerning his seed, and so Sarah, his wife, got involved and followed the local customs. Sarah asked Abraham to sleep with her maid, Hagar, but once Hagar conceived, Sarah drove her out into the desert.

And the angel of the LORD said unto her, Return to thy mistress, and submit thyself under her hands.

And the angel of the LORD said unto her, I will multiply thy seed exceedingly, that it shall not be numbered for multitude. And the angel of the LORD said unto her, Behold, thou art with child and shalt bear a son, and shalt call his name Ishmael; because the LORD hath heard thy affliction. And he will be a wild man; his hand will be against every man, and every man's hand against him; and he shall dwell in the presence of all his brethren.

—Genesis 16:9–12

After her encounter with the angel, Hagar returned to Abraham's household and had her son, whom she named Ishmael, and he would become the father of the Muslim nation.

Later, while Abraham was living at a place called Mamre, three strangers visited Abraham and astonished him. They told him that his wife, Sarah, who was old and never bore children, would soon have a son. Abraham believed the strangers, and a year later, Sarah gave birth to a boy child whose name was to be Isaac.

For a time, Abraham did what many of us have done; he allowed his circumstances to dictate his actions. Instead of seeing through the eye of promise, he saw only through the eye of circumstance. That's why the prophetic eye that God promised would come to this generation will be of vital importance to the entire body of

Christ in the days ahead. Jesus addressed this in these divulging instructions to His disciples:

The light of the body is the eye: if therefore thine eye be single, thy whole body shall be full of light. But if thine eye be evil, thy whole body shall be full of darkness. If therefore the light that is in thee be darkness, how great is that darkness!
—Matthew 6:22–23

From the loins of Abraham, Ishmael became the son of circumstance, an offspring of the situation. Isaac, however, became the son of promise and the offspring of faith. Who would have guessed that both these children, who were Abraham's sons, would one day make a lasting impression on the entire human population? Later, Abraham's faith was tested a second time when God asked him to sacrifice Isaac, the promised child, back to Him. By faith, Abraham proceeded to follow God's instructions without question. However, at the very last moment, God provided Himself with another sacrifice, a ram caught in the bush.

This was all done to show that Isaac and all who would operate under the dispensation of promise might be saved by the shed blood from a greater, eternal source.

For if the blood of bulls and goats, and the ashes of a heifer sprinkling the unclean, sanctifieth to the pu-

rifying of the flesh: How much more shall the blood
of Christ, who through the eternal Spirit offered
himself without spot to God, purge your conscience
from dead works to serve the living God?
—Hebrews 9:13–14

After the confirmation of Abraham's faith and obedi-
ence, God affirmed His covenant with him, promising
Abraham again many descendants, and that through
him, all nations would be blessed. Abraham's faith and
acceptance of God's terms established the first covenant
between the Jewish people and their God. This was all
done as a prelude to a much greater act with a much
greater purpose.

Behold, the days come, saith the LORD, that I will
make a new covenant with the house of Israel, and
with the house of Judah: Not according to the cove-
nant that I made with their fathers in the day that I
took them by the hand to bring them out of the land
of Egypt; which my covenant they brake, although I
was an husband unto them, saith the LORD.
—Jeremiah 31:31–32

Israel's moving away from their covenant with the
God that took them by the hand and brought them out
of the land of Egypt set in motion a chain of events that

would bring us to this remarkable place where we are today. A place where the proposed plan of God will herald itself through the prophetic messengers of this astounding declaration, as the name of Jesus will be lifted far above every principality, power, dominion, and might, and every name that is named not only in this world but in that which is to come.

I am the LORD: that is my name: and my glory will I not give to another, neither my praise to graven images. Behold, the former things are come to pass, and new things do I declare: before they spring forth I tell you of them.

—Isaiah 42:8–9

This decisive word from God, as it echoes down through time and in distant lands, continues to bring to the forefront this *engaging idea* of a people and their God doing great exploits together.

CHAPTER 10

When the Spirit Speaks

One of the most assuring aspects of our calling is that over and again, God has made it emphatically clear that this is not a journey that we've been asked to endure alone.

Howbeit when he, the Spirit of truth, is come, he will guide you into all truth: for he shall not speak of himself; but whatsoever he shall hear, that shall he speak: and he will shew you things to come.

—John 16:13

For our betterment, we are entreated to follow a sound prophetic directive coming from the mouth of Christ Himself. It's imperative that we allow the Spirit to show us where we really are rather than indulge us in our notions of where we'd prefer to be. God has already determined that His people shall become a budding example to the nations.

All ye inhabitants of the world, and dwellers on the earth, see ye, when he lifteth up an ensign on the mountains; and when he bloweth a trumpet, hear ye.

—Isaiah 18:3

With Christ and the cross as our ensign, by His Spirit, God is leading us toward an enormous prophetic utterance, one that the entire world will not be able to ignore, *"...when He bloweth a trumpet, hear ye."* This utterance will be the first fruits of those who are both able to see and hear, *"...but whatsoever he shall hear, that shall he speak: and he will shew you things to come."* Webster defines *ensign* as "a flag, banner, or symbol of authority." There is a sense, however, that no group with the kind of humble and unassuming history as the true Church has had would be interested in carrying that kind of a banner or responsibility. Just as the work that God is performing among many in the world today has yet to be completed, God's work in, around, and through His chosen is also still a work in progress.

It's apparent that God has a plan for His beloved offspring that goes beyond her ability to totally comprehend, but the fact remains that through all her ups and downs, God has never taken his eyes off that which He has declared by covenant to be His own.

The Spirit itself beareth witness with our spirit, that we are the children of God.

—Romans 8:16

However, this seal upon Abraham's seed (which would ultimately become the offspring of God through Christ) would prove to be both a blessing and a curse. Though God was always with her, for some of God's elect, this is one truth that was sometimes hard to swallow as, down through the centuries, her enemies had grown in increasing numbers with devastating campaigns such as the Crusades, which were a series of religious wars that took place in the Holy Land between 1095 and 1271 in part to try and take control of Jerusalem, and the horrible Inquisitions, which also took place between 1184 and the 1230s, initiated by a group of institutions demanding loyalty to the Catholic Church. It was during those times that a huge untold number of Jewish and Christian lives would be lost, a period that would ultimately become known as the Dark Ages.

It is not always easy to make the case to those who oppose us that we are heirs to God's bountiful inheritance, but the Scriptures are filled with God's profound response to this human form of inductive reasoning.

For every beast of the forest is mine, and the cattle upon a thousand hills. I know all the fowls of the mountains: and the wild beasts of the field are mine. If I were hungry, I would not tell thee: for the world is mine, and the fulness thereof.

—Psalm 50:10–12

Though the implementation of God's blueprint for our distinct positioning and renown often seemed futile or unavailing, our future as lively stones before the nations was never truly threatened.

> *Ye also, as lively stones, are built up a spiritual house, an holy priesthood, to offer up spiritual sacrifices, acceptable to God by Jesus Christ. Wherefore also it is contained in the scripture, Behold, I lay in Sion a chief corner stone, elect, precious: and he that believeth on him shall not be confounded.*
>
> —1 Peter 2:5–6

All through the Scriptures, we are given prophetic forecasts, earmarks, and inevitable signals as to how this preconceived movement of God would end up. The prophetic movement is the most original and potent expression of Christian thought, and if one were open to the voice of the Spirit, they would find in unprecedented detail, glimpses into our future exploits through this supernatural medium.

But the people that do know their God shall be strong, and do exploits.

—Daniel 11:32

Possibly, the most celebrated of all of Israel's kings was King David, whose name meant "beloved." David certainly held a special place in the heart of God. He was the second king of the united kingdom of the Hebrew people after King Saul. As a young boy, he was the keeper of his father's sheep and showed a great deal of courage and faithfulness by killing both a lion and a bear that tried to attack the flock. Young David also displayed an outstanding musical talent with the harp, a fact that figured prominently in his life.

And it came to pass, when the evil spirit from God was upon Saul, that David took an harp, and played with his hand: so Saul was refreshed, and was well, and the evil spirit departed from him.

—1 Samuel 16:23

When Saul was rejected by God as king, the prophet Samuel went to Bethlehem to anoint David as the future king of Israel. David, an ancestor of Jesus Christ and writer of numerous songs, lived a life filled with one adventurous or notable incident after another.

And David was afraid of God that day, saying, How
shall I bring the ark of God home to me? So David
brought not the ark home to himself to the city of
David, but carried it aside into the house of Obed-
edom the Gittite. And the ark of God remained with
the family of Obededom in his house three months.
And the LORD blessed the house of Obededom, and
all that he had.

—1 Chronicles 13:12–14

After reading this Scripture, I received a startling revelation that in some cases, when that which represents the command of God is not located in its rightful place, those who are in possession of it can still benefit from its presence.

The scribes and the Pharisees sit in Moses' seat: All there-
fore whatsoever they bid you observe, that observe and do; but
do not ye after their works: for they say, and do not.

—Matthew 23:2–3

This was indeed an in-season revelation. Like prophecies, all revelations do not always take place in the season in which they were given. This was certainly a heart-wrenching occurrence for David and all Israel. They had finally retrieved from the Philistines the most sacred ark of the covenant. This was to represent the presence of God in their midst. It was a brief time of great celebration. The joy and exuberance that these people shared were awe-inspiring as one reads this biblical account of what was to be one of Israel's finest moments.

When the cart carrying the ark reached a certain point and the oxen stumbled, Uzza put forth his hand to hold the ark, and God took his life. Apparently, this man, Uzza, not being a priest, should have never laid his hands upon that which was most sacred to God.

Being shocked, confused, and afraid to bring the ark to himself, David instead took it aside to the house of Obed-Edom, who was possibly one of his bodyguards. Here is an interesting note; the Bible tells us that although the ark was not in its proper place (that is to say in Israel's possession) for three months, the house of Obed-Edom prospered.

The fact that those who hold fast to staunch legalistic tradition have enjoyed worldwide recognition and have certainly prospered in an often-boastful way from their statute as the voices of the Christian Church does not mean that God is content with complacency.

Just as David and all Israel believed that the very presence of the ark in their midst was confirmation that God was with them, so do we believe today that once the Spirit of exposition speaks and is upheld through prophetic discernment, so will it also stand as our assurance that God is with us.

Thus all Israel brought up the ark of the covenant of the LORD with shouting, and with sound of the cornet, and with trumpets, and with cymbals, making a noise with psalteries and harps.

—1 Chronicles 15:28

Even though David himself lived in a king's house and wore fine linen, his passion for retrieving the ark so that all Israel could be blessed never faltered.

But ye shall receive power, after that the Holy Ghost is come upon you: and ye shall be witnesses unto me both in Jerusalem, and in all Judaea, and in Samaria, and unto the uttermost part of the earth.

—Acts 1:8

Using David and all Israel as our example, we should incorporate that same passion and determination in order that we too might recover that which was lost. It is our hope that all Christians might see this for what it is, not just a mere suggestion or plea from God but an opportunity to be witnesses and recipients of the most abundant outpouring of His presence this generation has ever seen. One filled with power and heightened anticipation of the greatest event that this world has ever known—the second coming of our blessed Messiah and Lord, Jesus Christ.

> *And the apostles and brethren that were in Judaea heard that the Gentiles had also received the word of God. And when Peter was come up to Jerusalem, they that were of the circumcision contended with him, saying, Thou wentest in to men uncircumcised, and didst eat with them.*
>
> —Acts 11:1–3

This Scripture goes on to tell us that the apostle Peter, a Jew, rehearsed this same matter in the spirit of revelation and expounded it by order. He explained to them what had happened and why he had conducted himself in the manner that he did. And that it was, in fact, a new day.

We must be willing to reach out to those who are currently undecided about the future direction of their lives and of the Church. Be it the corporate executive, the man next door, or the broken and disenfranchised brother or sister on the street. We must let them know that all the barriers, challenges, false starts, and missteps that appear to be persistent in making life meaningless can and will be confronted in a new way. We now have access to the formula for blessings, our returning to the illuminating word that God had set in place before the foundation of the world.

So shall my word be that goeth forth out of my mouth: It shall not return unto me void, but it shall accomplish that which I please, and it shall prosper in the thing whereto I send it.

—Isaiah 55:11

And so it shall be, with the voice and resurgence of the Spirit of Truth standing as a beacon of hope to all who are willing to follow this elevated pathway laid out by His Spirit.

As through it all, whenever the time was right, by way of a prophetic discourse, God never ceased to bolster our walk of faith as we endeavor to keep cadence on an uncharted journey towards a divine legacy.

Behold, the former things are come to pass, and new things do I declare: before they spring forth I tell you of them.

—Isaiah 42:9

For the vision is yet for an appointed time, but at the end it shall speak, and not lie: though it tarry, wait for it; because it will surely come, it will not tarry.

—Habakkuk 2:3

What a captivating thought that through dreams and visions, God would ignite in us a force to be reckoned with, *"...but at the end it shall speak, and not lie..."* This concludes that the stuff we are made of will not be the result of His permissive will but rather His divine will. From this reckoning force, *a profound word*; shackles will be broken, and strongholds will be torn down. All because the verdict is in, and all who have been pardoned by the blood have been found not guilty.

For ever, O LORD, thy word is settled in heaven. Thy faithfulness is unto all generations.

—Psalm 119:89–90

CHAPTER 11

Identifying Symbols of Prophecy

O magnify the LORD with me, and let us exalt his name to-gether. I sought the LORD, and he heard me, and delivered me from all my fears. They looked unto him, and were lightened: and their faces were not ashamed.

—Psalm 34:3–5

This psalm was written by King David concerning an incident where he was captured by the Philistine king, Achish, while being pursued by those of the house of King Saul. David's plan of escape was definitely a unique one. Immediately after being captured, David "feigned himself mad," which turned out to be a good idea. Once it was determined by the king that David was not a threat, nor was he in possession of the mental faculties to cause any future problems, David was released. Now the one question that will go unanswered is, whose idea was it to fake madness, David's or God's? David, who feared for his life, wrote, *"I sought the LORD, and he heard me, and delivered me from all my fears."* For most people, it's difficult to fathom God operating outside of the box even though He is the Creator not only of the box, but all its perimeters.

O the depth of the riches both of the wisdom and knowledge of God! how unsearchable are his judgments, and his ways past finding out!

—Romans 11:33

This chapter is simply an extension of the movement we just shared in "When the Spirit Speaks" and our quest toward identifying symbols of prophecy. I must admit that I really enjoyed this voyage into God's circle of intense knowledge.

God, who at sundry times and in divers manners spake in time past unto the fathers by the prophets, hath in these last days spoken unto us by his Son, whom he hath appointed heir of all things, by whom also he made the worlds.

—Hebrews 1:1–2

God has acclimated the hearts and minds of those chosen to know and hear His voice. Jesus Himself established that as a sign or symbol to those in training who followed Him and often sat at His feet.

And the disciples came, and said unto him, why speakest thou unto them in parables? He answered and said unto them, Because it is given unto you to know the mysteries of the kingdom of heaven, but to them it is not given.
—Matthew 13:10–11

In answering His disciples, Jesus made it clear that there would be those connected to a certain frequency that many might long to hear from or tap in to but would be unable to do so.

But it is written, Eye hath not seen, nor ear heard, neither have entered into the heart of man, the things which God hath prepared for them that love him. But God hath revealed them unto us by his Spirit: for the Spirit searcheth all things, yea, the deep things of God.
—1 Corinthians 2:9–10

Jesus' parables were filled with symbols. When rightly discerned in someone's dreams or visions today, they are easily identifiable.

And Jesus answered and spake unto them again by parables, and said, The kingdom of heaven is

*like unto a certain king, which made a marriage
for his son, and sent forth his servants to call them
that were bidden to the wedding: and they would
not come. Again, he sent forth other servants, saying, Tell them which are bidden, Behold, I have
prepared my dinner: my oxen and my fatlings are
killed, and all things are ready: come unto the marriage. But they made light of it, and went their
ways, one to his farm, another to his merchandise:
And the remnant took his servants, and entreated
them spitefully, and slew them. But when the king
heard thereof, he was wroth: and he sent forth his
armies, and destroyed those murderers, and burned
up their city. Then saith he to his servants, The wedding is ready, but they which were bidden were not
worthy. Go ye therefore into the highways, and as
many as ye shall find, bid to the marriage. So those
servants went out into the highways, and gathered
together all as many as they found, both bad and
good: and the wedding was furnished with guests.*
—Matthew 22:1–10

A certain king in a dream would represent wealth,
power, and popularity. A wedding or marriage connotes
a new beginning or transition in life. A feast represents
abundance, indulging and enjoying oneself. A cow or
oxen describes a creature that is deeply connected to

the earth. They slew them; death generally symbolizes some kind of change, the end of one thing and the beginning of something new. The angry king burned up the city. A fire usually represents anger and aggression that's out of control, and it could cause total destruction. A wedding garment or gown is a sign of the coming of a comfortable and thriving lifestyle, or it signals accomplishment or the fulfillment that comes from achieving a long-time goal.

In this recent dream, all over the world, the ground is shaking, and people are unable to keep their balance. Everywhere the dreamer looks, folks are lying down, and no matter how hard others try to help, the situation appears to be getting worse. In the middle of all this sickness, there's a tall tree with no leaves on it. The sun is very hot, but the tree doesn't provide any shade. As the people offer aid to each other, whatever they have contracted only spreads and adds to the suffering of those around them. When the dreamer surveys this horrendous occurrence, all they can do is sit in a corner and weep in silence.

In this dream, the world symbolizes a global event. The shaking represents uncertainty, ambiguity, obscurity, and an unhinging of things as they currently are. The people lying down and the inability to help, along with the spreading of the malady, all fall under a symbol of weakness. The notions of being lost or without answers are usually accompanied by feelings of frustration and confusion. The tall tree offers intimidation, insecurity, and feelings of being overwhelmed by a certain situation or person. However, the fact that the tree offered no shade is not unlike a dream with a wild beast with no teeth; they both have more bark than bite; though graphic in appearance, they offer no real threat to the situation. The silent weeping falls under the symbol of soft sounds, which are a sign of absolution or tears and hope for a better day. Colors can also have significant meanings.

Come now, and let us reason together, saith the LORD: though your sins be as scarlet, they shall be as white as snow; though they be red like crimson, they shall be as wool.
—Isaiah 1:18

Crimson, scarlet, or red symbolizes raw energy, force, vigor, intense passion, and aggression. Note the prior coordination of this group before grace showed up. White reflects justice, goodness, perfection, truth, completion of works. Blue suggests truth, wisdom, tranquility, heaven, eternity, devotion, loyalty, and openness. Black represents danger, unknown, unconsciousness, mystery, darkness, and sometimes even death.

Now, I submit to you that those given foresight and an acute sense of visualization can easily recognize these symbols and discern how they can be applied to certain settings.

For every one that useth milk is unskillful in the word of righteousness: for he is a babe. But strong meat belongeth to them that are of full age, even those who by reason of use have their senses exercised to discern both good and evil.

—Hebrews 5:13–14

In the Old Testament book of 2 Kings, the servant of Elisha, the prophet, was frightened because the king of Syria had sent his army against them.

And he answered, Fear not: for they that be with us are more than they that be with them. And Elisha prayed, and said, LORD, I pray thee, open his eyes, that he may see. And the LORD opened the eyes of the young man; and he saw: and, behold, the mountain was full of horses and chariots of fire round about Elisha.

—2 Kings 6:16–17

Often, God will allow conditions to occur requiring the aid of a seer. So that others might know that God's seer is not alone. I certainly see that happening soon; in fact, with some, it's happening already.

And Pharaoh said unto Joseph, I have dreamed a dream, and there is none that can interpret it: and I have heard say of thee, that thou canst understand a dream to interpret it. And Joseph answered Pharaoh, saying, It is not in me: God shall give Pharaoh an answer of peace.

—Genesis 41:15–16

The King Nebuchadnezzar had a troubling dream that neither he nor his wise men, astrologers, magicians, or soothsayers could interpret, but Daniel assured him that there was a God in heaven who could reveal all things to those whom He would.

The king answered and said to Daniel, whose name was Belteshazzar, Art thou able to make known unto me the dream which I have seen, and the interpretation thereof? Daniel answered in the presence of the king, and said, The secret which the king hath demanded cannot the wise men, the astrologers, the magicians, the soothsayers, shew unto the king; but there is a God in heaven that revealeth secrets, and maketh known to the king Nebuchadnezzar what shall be in the latter days. Thy dream, and the visions of thy head upon thy bed are these.

—Daniel 2:26–28

The Bible goes on to tell us that the king fell on his face and worshiped Daniel and commanded that he should be given gifts. You'll be surprised at how grateful some folk may become when you are able to see them out of an unsettling situation.

The king answered unto Daniel, and said, Of a truth it is, that your God is a God of gods, and a Lord of kings, and a revealer of secrets, seeing thou couldest reveal this secret.

—Daniel 2:47

These astonishing displays of God's preeminence and power will often cause the most hardened skeptics and many who rebel against God to come to a place of humility.

And Jonah began to enter into the city a day's journey, and he cried, and said, Yet forty days, and Nineveh shall be overthrown. So the people of Nineveh believed God, and proclaimed a fast, and put on sackcloth, from the greatest of them even to the least of them. And God saw their works, that they turned from their evil way; and God repented of the evil, that he had said that he would do unto them; and he did it not.

—Jonah 3:4–5, 10

One of the many things that God shows His mastery at is His incredible ability to recover plights and situations long after they have passed the *"point of no return."* While everyone else has thrown up their hands and abandoned all hopes that this particular predicament could ever see the light of day, God shows up, and as if to reverse time, He brings about the kinds of results that would cause those who witness it to sit in awe and wonder what just happened. These kinds of amazing feats that are so faith-inspiring cause those of us who have experienced these life-changing events to cry from the depths of our souls all praises to the one true and living God. Isaiah the Prophet has enlightened us to the fact that God is indeed the Architect and Designer of both good and evil. So, we need not ask what gives God the right, power, and authority to do these kinds of things.

I form the light, and create darkness: I make peace, and create evil: I the LORD do all these things.
—Isaiah 45:7

Now, I know to some that it might seem to be a dismal or bleak thing to consider, but the Bible tells us that God chastens those that He loves. Sometimes, He has a way of making us uncomfortable to move us toward His divine design.

Beloved, think it not strange concerning the fiery trial which is to try you, as though some strange thing happened unto you: But rejoice, inasmuch as ye are partakers of Christ's sufferings; that, when his glory shall be revealed, ye may be glad also with exceeding joy.

—1 Peter 4:12–13

Blessed are ye, when men shall revile you, and persecute you, and shall say all manner of evil against you falsely, for my sake. Rejoice, and be exceeding glad: for great is your reward in heaven: for so persecuted they the prophets which were before you.

—Matthew 5:11–12

These words were spoken by Jesus to a group who were under heavy persecution inflicted upon them by the Roman dictatorship. Needless to say, His words probably seemed a little insensitive when it came to addressing their current situation.

Once again, you can sense God operating within His own time frame, as He clearly contemplates or nurtures a broader agenda. This agenda extends far beyond our individual priorities or what works best for us at the moment. And so it is, with the dreamers and visionaries acting out God's objective in these *"last days,"* I am convinced that unlike any time in recent history, they, through this "new thing," will have a lasting effect and impact on the lives of so many.

Let a man so account of us, as of the ministers of Christ, and stewards of the mysteries of God.

—1 Corinthians 4:1

This thunderous, earth-shaking clarion call to what God has so amply and candidly introduced as His "new thing" with its entire synergistic boldness will be highlighted and gracefully embodied standing with God against His enemies, both spiritual and natural.

And they went forth, and preached every where, the Lord working with them, and confirming the word with signs following.

—Mark 16:20

As we move forward, we will be able to identify the similarities between both the new and old prophets and the irrefutable kinship they have with each other.

Though thy beginning was small, yet thy latter end should greatly increase.

—Job 8:7

Although we have churches on almost every corner, as a people of one body, too many have never looked toward heaven for answers. We walked away from our most substantial resource—God. It is my contention that as a chosen generation and as a part of His elect remnant, we must return to Him and seek His endowment. There are just too many negative forces at work for us to try and go it alone. More importantly, we must all understand that our greater concerns are no longer just a matter of differences between race or ideology. Our immediate apprehensions must be broader and inclusive in scope.

When the people who were responsible for the Trade Center bombings set out to bring those buildings down, not once did they consider who might have been inside. There were Whites, Blacks, Jews, Asians, Mexicans, and even Muslims, but to our enemies, it was all about the spilling of that one blood.

We all know that there is a lot of realigning of support that must take place, but with clear *God-given* direction, we can learn to accept and respect all that He has given us.

Now there are diversities of gifts, but the same Spirit. And there are differences of administrations, but the same Lord. And there are diversities of operations, but it is the same God which worketh all in all.

—1 Corinthians 12:4–6

Even so then at this present time also there is a remnant according to the election of grace.

—Romans 11:5

Truly, we bless and praise God for that remnant, along with the prophetic signs and symbols produced by the dreamers and visionaries in this critical and, more importantly, decisive hour.

CHAPTER 12

Lift Up Your Heads

See that ye refuse not him that speaketh. For if they escaped not who refused him that spake on earth, much more shall not we escape, if we turn away from him that speaketh from heaven: Whose voice then shook the earth: but now he hath promised, saying, Yet once more I shake not the earth only, but also heaven.

—Hebrews 12:25–26

Now, as we previously noted, God is adamant over the fact that for this generation, there will be a fundamental shaking that will be difficult if not impossible to ignore. *"See that [you] refuse not him that speaketh."* It also appears that these events will be accompanied by words of caution and prior notification.

Since the tragedy of 9/11 in Manhattan, across the Middle East, Russia, China, and Europe, the world has been holding its breath in the wake of one explosive event after another. From one side of the globe to the other, nature has been shaking the very foundation of our planet with hurricanes, tsunamis, volcanic eruptions, earthquakes, firestorms, and melting ice. Every day, more of our wildlife, rain forests, and ice caps are starting to disappear. The health of our global economy remains uncertain. Billions of dollars, euros, and pounds are being lost or mismanaged by large corporations at an alarming rate, taking with them the savings of millions of people. That is why we can no longer afford a form of godliness that has no power; because if there ever was a time for fervent effectual prayer in the Church, it's now. Our hope is that the chosen of God be prompted to give rise to those amazing prophetic proclamations being revealed to them by God's own Spirit.

If the Church remained consistent with the teachings of Christ, especially while it was being managed by those being led by the Spirit of Truth, such as the apostles Peter and Paul, there would not be a lot of room for imaginary and speculative thinking. But when the Church found her largest constituency among the Greeks and especially the mystical unbalance of the Greeks of Asia Minor, all sorts of strange opinions and theories arose and grew to power.

When it was determined by the dictates and actions of the Spirit that a Gentile did not have to convert to Judaism to become a follower of Christ, this opened the door to widespread church growth among the Gentiles.

So many Gentiles were saved that the Jewish believer became a minority. However, history shows that as the center of the Christian faith was moved from "Jerusalem to Rome," it became increasingly Hellenized, adopting pagan customs and philosophies rather than the God-ordained practices and beliefs we now find in the Bible. At the same time, Christianity became increasingly anti-Jewish. By 135 AD, the Romans renamed Israel "Syria-Palestine." The New Testament uses the land of Israel twice (Matthew 2:20–21) but never uses the name "Palestine" or "Palestinian."

By 306 AD, Constantine, a Roman emperor, came into power. He was a master politician. He tried to attract heathens to Christianity by modifying pagan customs and festivals and giving them Christian meanings. This would still allow Christians to keep their traditions. The group he did not like was the Jews since they had rebelled against Rome. The Church was more than willing to follow Constantine's lead to avoid persecution. Constantine built many churches and monasteries, but the Jews were not permitted in Jerusalem except for one day a year. On this day, they were allowed to mourn the destruction of the temple.

Even with these historical atrocities, there was always this emerging vibration or persistent conviction that somehow, their champion was preparing for His celebrated entrance, all the while being encouraged by the cheering songs and aspirations of those who would love His appearing.

> *Lift up your heads, O ye gates; and be ye lift up, ye everlasting doors; and the King of glory shall come in. Who is this King of glory? The LORD strong and mighty, the LORD mighty in battle.*
>
> —Psalm 24:7–8

Also, during Emperor Constantine's reign, he would express the anti-Judaic sentiments of the bishops of the Church world when he wrote:

> *Let us therefore have nothing in common with this odious people the Jews, for we have received from our savior a different way. Strive and pray continually that the purity of your souls may not be sullied by fellowship with the customs of these most wicked men... all should unite in desiring that which sound reason appears to demand in avoiding all participation in the perjured conduct of the Jews.*[2]

Prior to Constantine's rhetoric, *"...for we have received from our savior a different way...,"* the apostle Paul wrote:

---

2 "Constantine the Great and Judaism," Wikipedia, last modified March 26, 2021, https://en.wikipedia.org/wiki/Constantine_the_Great_and_Judaism.

But though we, or an angel from heaven, preach any other gospel unto you than that which we have preached unto you, let him be accursed. As we said before, so say I now again, if any man preach any other gospel unto you than that ye have received, let him be accursed.

—Galatians 1:8–9

Paul asserts that without an unconditional, long-standing word from God, there would be no Christian Church. That's why we do thank God for His enduring Church and our link to her remarkable history. And most of all, because that grand entrance did take place.

And a very great multitude spread their garments in the way; others cut down branches from the trees, and strawed them in the way. And the multitudes that went before, and that followed, cried, saying, Hosanna to the son of David: Blessed is he that cometh in the name of the Lord; Hosanna in the highest.

—Matthew 21:8–9

In the Gospel of John, chapter 7, Jesus celebrates the Feast of Tabernacles; in that same Gospel of John, chapter 10, Jesus is in the temple for Hanukkah or Passover; it is the feast that signified the fact that Jesus was killed for the redemption of all men.

And the blood shall be to you for a token upon the houses where ye are: and when I see the blood, I will pass over you.

—Exodus 12:13

The word "token" here literally means "a sign or promise of future events."

We are told to celebrate *"the feast"* in 1 Corinthians 5:8. The Feast of Early Fruits is the feast that symbolizes Jesus being raised from the dead. "Pentecost," which means "fifty" and denotes a celebration of liberation from slavery held every fifty years (Jubilee), is the feast in which the Holy Spirit was sent to baptize the believers. People in Jerusalem during Shavuot or Pentecost were amazed that the 120 who were all Galileans spoke about God in different languages (Acts 2:7), which certifies the fact that when God wants to be heard, He will be heard. And as an added bonus, there's no way you can lift God up and not be elevated as well.

For this reason, God gives voice to Himself through the prophetic tongues of those whom He has chosen. There are a lot of folks that see God as just words on a page, but because He has allowed us to rehearse the matter with Him, up close and personal, we know that it's never iffy with His conclusions. In fact, the only thing God has ever promised to forget, once we give our lives over to His call, is our sins. That's why you can rest assured that when the time is right, He's going to make a noise, and for you and me, that time is now.

In the book of Judges, we are introduced to another chosen vessel that went by the name of Samson. His mother was barren, but because God decided to use a dead womb, the shackles of shame and the bondage of ridicule were removed. Samson's mother was allowed to experience a kind of freedom she had never known before. The Bible says an angel came and began to etch out plans for a pregnancy that had not yet taken place. Through a prophetic arrangement, new life was about to spring forth, which simply meant that this woman, just like many of you, was allowed to recapture an event that had played out in the mind of God many times before.

And the angel of the LORD appeared unto the woman, and said unto her, Behold now, thou art barren, and bearest not: but thou shalt conceive, and bear a son.

—Judges 13:3

As the story goes on, we find this brother, Samson, was literally chained to a set of daunting circumstances.

And when the people saw him, they praised their god: for they said, Our god hath delivered into our hands our enemy, and the destroyer of our country, which slew many of us.

—Judges 16:24

These people literally thought that because they took Samson's stuff, his God went bankrupt and had abandoned him. But the Bible makes it clear that Samson's strength had nothing to do with his bronze or mass, but it was a gift from God. And just like any gift that God gives, it's going to come with a warranty. This is something that we all must remember moving forward.

For the gifts and calling of God are without repentance.
—Romans 11:29

You should never express regret for any gift that God has given you. But in order to bless others, you must remain committed to your vocation as you walk and operate under the shadow of that anointing.

Therefore, my beloved brethren, be ye steadfast, unmovable, always abounding in the work of the Lord, forasmuch as ye know that your labour is not in vain in the Lord.
—1 Corinthians 15:58

Samson had the reality of God's divine person birthed in his heart; therefore, he knew that he could become victorious just by reminding himself of the level of God's mercy and the power of His love.

Through the word of faith, God persistently hammered home His agenda, one that Jesus would reiterate in His prayer to the Father.

And this is life eternal, that they might know thee the only true God, and Jesus Christ, whom thou hast sent.

—John 17:3

Peter and Andrew are the first two Jewish fishermen to follow Jesus; they lived in Galilee. The next two followers of Jesus were James and John, also fishermen from Galilee. Phillip, Bartholomew, Thomas, Matthew, Samuel, Thaddeus, Simon, and Judas were among them as well.

Although they often met with ridicule and threats from the local authorities, these men developed tunnel vision when it came to following in steps of the *Big Fisherman.*

And the word of God increased; and the number of the disciples multiplied in Jerusalem greatly; and a great company of the priests were obedient to the faith.

—Acts 6:7

Acts 15 highlights the council members who met in Jerusalem to figure out how to include the Gentiles in the Church. By verse 22, a letter had been drafted to the Gentile believers about the requirements for following Jesus. In Acts 21, Paul arrives in Jerusalem to see James and the elders of the Church. Paul reveals to them what

God had done among the Gentiles, and this was their response, "You see, brother, how many thousands of Jews have believed, and all of them are zealous for the law."

We must alert *a sleeping church*, through prophetic insight, that it was no coincidence that when the authentic Jewish heritage of the Church was replaced with paganism, intimacy with God was watered down. The supernatural power of God was replaced with the politics and traditions of men. When the Church walked away from its historical roots, it abandoned God's pattern. And the original Church split would be the division between Jew and Gentile.

Love worketh no ill to his neighbour: therefore love is the fulfilling of the law. And that, knowing the time, that now it is high time to awake out of sleep: for now is our salvation nearer than when we believed.

—Romans 13:10–11

We should let the wisdom of this statement from the apostle Paul serve as a warning to us to use caution as we approach the non-Christian Jews, those who insist on protecting the traditions and beliefs passed down through generations. Be mindful that the strength of their argument can be extracted from the character, attitude, and history of the *so-called* Christian Church.

This was a Church that began with Jews and Gentiles walking hand in hand, promoting an idea that they collectively had embraced and exercised. Later, the same Church that many Jews gave rise, credence, and their lives to would be turned into a deadly sword against them, leaving both groups in a state of increased vulnerability.

Two are better than one; because they have a good reward for their labour. For if they fall, the one will lift up his fellow: but woe to him that is alone when he falleth; for he hath not another to help him up.
—Ecclesiastes 4:9–10

Constantine retained some of the heathen titles of the emperor as that of "pontifex maximus," which means "chief priest," both the head of the empire and the head of the Church as well, a title, by the way, held by all of the popes since. Because of his strategies and political savvy, the city of Rome was replaced by Constantinople, which is now Istanbul, as the capital of the world.

During that same period, however, the Roman Church was growing in prestige and power, and the bishop of Rome, now entitled pope, was claiming the throne of authority over the entire Christian world. All during these turbulent times, however, the people of God continued to call on Him for their day in court.

> *When the LORD shall build up Zion, he shall appear in his glory. He will regard the prayer of the destitute, and not despise their prayer. This shall be written for the generation to come: and the people which shall be created shall praise the LORD.*
>
> —Psalm 102:16–18

As everywhere, bishops controlled the churches, but the question that was constantly arising was, who should control the bishops? What bishop would take the place of the emperor over the Church?

The presiding bishops in certain cities soon came to be called "metropolitans" and afterward, "patriarchs." There were patriarchs at Jerusalem, Antioch, Alexander, Constantinople, and Rome. The Roman bishop took the title of "papa," "father," later changed to pope.

Between these five patriarchs were frequent contests, but the question finally narrowed down to the choice between the patriarch of Constantinople and the pope of Rome as head of the Church. In the end, Rome presented the greatest argument. Rome was the only Church that named as its founders two apostles, Peter and Paul, both Jews. The contention was that Peter was the first bishop of Rome, and so he must have been "papa," "father," or pope.

But Peter was present when Jesus spoke these words in the book of Matthew.

And call no man your father upon the earth: for one is your Father, which is in heaven.
                                                        —Matthew 23:9

Although the apostle Peter did spend time with the church in Rome, we know that his ending was a lot less glamorous than that of a pope.

The beginning of the seventh century found Jews inhabiting most areas in Europe. I believe here that a distinction should be made between two terms: "exile," which means "a compulsory banishment," and "Diaspora," which signifies "a voluntary scattering." Both have been part of Jewish existence from their earliest history. Exile became Diaspora when the Jews adjusted themselves to their new environment.

The Jews had first arrived in Europe in the wake of the conquering Roman legions, but now it had become increasingly difficult for the Jews to navigate successfully through the turbulent wars of the newly converted and newly fanatic European nations. Once again, what the Jews of Europe would learn was consistent with their past and what would turn out to be consistent with much of their future. Just when they began to feel at home anywhere else but Israel, what they would be experiencing would be nothing more than the calm before the storm.

In order to remain rooted in what they believed to be a divine bloodline, they would constantly remind themselves of their heritage and who it was that kept them.

The LORD is my strength and song, and he is become my salvation: he is my God, and I will prepare him an habitation; my father's God, and I will exalt him.

—Exodus 15:2

The high level of persecution that had to be endured in the seventh century led to the almost total devastation of Spanish Jewry. It is astonishing that so many Jews clung to their own values. Nothing less than an unshakable conviction of moral and religious faith could have enabled them to survive the relentless wave of terror and forced conversions—*convert or die.* During that same period in the Middle East, the two chief towns of Arabia were Mecca and Medina. Mecca, more than a trading center, was the site of the Kabba, a small temple of black stone, the cornerstone of which was a meteorite—and as such, it was a center of religious pilgrimage.

Medina at that time was a smaller city founded, it is said, by Jews who had originally come there from Yemen. Until 525 AD, the princes of Medina had for centuries professed Judaism as their religion. It was against this backdrop that the career of the prophet Moham-med unfolded. Born in Mecca during the (Christian) era of poor humble stock, Mohammed rose from a mere camel driver to become first the leader of a caravan and then the leader of the entire Arab people. It is said that Mohammed was intrigued by the religious beliefs of both Jews and Christians.

Mohammed felt himself possessed of prophetic power, a power whose supernatural provision was confirmed by occasional visitations from heaven. He saw himself uniting in his person two distinct func-tions, that of the prophet and that of the apostle. His earlier followers were slaves and people of humble origin. The well-to-do shunned him and saw him as a threat to their way of life, and they began to confront him aggressively. In 622 CE, fearing for his life, Mo-hammed fled with a few close followers to Medina. The date of this flight, known in Arabic as the Bejira, marks the beginning of the Muslim calendar.

In arriving at Medina, he met with unexpected re-sistance from the Jews. Angered by their opposition and jealous of their financial success, Mohammed con-ceived a hatred for Jews. To propagate or spawn his new religion of Islam, Mohammed selected a novel method. Most of his converts were won on the field of battle where the beaten, usually members of trading caravans from Mecca, were given the alternative to convert or die. And still today, "Death to Israel and all her infidel allies" is the battle cry that burns within the hearts of Islamic extremists across the globe, never understanding that their fight is not just against a certain people or group but against a master objective that spans the entire length of time itself complete with its own implacable barriers of protection.

When thou passest through the waters, I will be with thee; and through the rivers, they shall not overflow thee: when thou walkest through the fire, thou shalt not be burned; neither shall the flame kindle upon thee.

—Isaiah 43:2

Just as in the beginning, Adam's son Cain slew his brother, Abel, in a jealous rage because of the apparent favor of God that was upon Abel's life; Islamic extremists are convinced that if the Jews exist, they will never receive their rightful place as rulers of the Middle East and eventually the entire world. To this end, they will align themselves with anyone who shares their commitment to bring Israel to a place of total extinction. Ishmael the Approved against Isaac the Appointed to whom God has said:

For I know the thoughts that I think toward you, saith the LORD, thoughts of peace, and not of evil, to give you an expected end.

—Jeremiah 29:11

Therefore, the conclusion of the matter is that no counter effort can ever be successful against that which God has already ordained. Not even by a powerful, influential religious group such as radical Islam, although in their hearts and minds they have sworn to stop at nothing to reach their goal, which is the destruction of Israel and her allies in the West.

This is the purpose that is purposed upon the whole earth: and this is the hand that is stretched out upon all the nations. For the LORD of hosts hath purposed, and who shall disannul it? and his hand is stretched out, and who shall turn it back?

—Isaiah 14:26–27

This is the same kind of fervor and dedication that the Christian Church must have as she embarks on her campaign. We must acknowledge these links and recognize the divine wisdom of God that has been set before us. God has made it emphatically clear that our greatest blessings lie before us, a blessing replete with well-grounded accounts of where we began, where we are, and, more importantly, where we are headed.

Unlike any time in its recent history, the church must prepare itself for a different type of warfare. One being led by those who, through faith, prayer, dreams, and visions, are able to see before them a well-orchestrated plan and a confirmed conquest. All glory to the one true and living God.

Ye are of God, little children, and have overcome them: because greater is he that is in you, than he that is in the world.
—1 John 4:4

Herein rests a truth that can never be ignored, that our Bible, filled with so many infallible proofs of the linkage between those who began and have brought us to this place, where we can and will begin again, remains the number-one bestseller of all times.

For the word of God is quick, and powerful, and sharper than any twoedged sword, piercing even to the dividing asunder of soul and spirit, and of the joints and marrow, and is a discerner of the thoughts and intents of the heart.
—Hebrews 4:12

CHAPTER 13

Quitting is Not an Option

And in thy seed shall all the nations of the earth be blessed;
because thou hast obeyed my voice.

—Genesis 22:18

When God promised Abraham that *"...in thy seed shall all nations of the earth be blessed...,"* He set in motion a chain of events that would have a significant bearing on the lives of those of His calling for thousands of years. Although, as with so many others before and after him, Abraham was never fully aware of the scope of this massive creative masterpiece that God had fashioned according to His good pleasure and would carry out in the manner of His divine authority and His excellent greatness. In doing so, God initiated a course of action that would span the entire human landscape, taking both men and women from natural creation to eternal salvation. Not only would this covenant be etched in granite, the Ten Commandments, but also be signed in blood that was drawn from Emmanuel's veins.

Now to Abraham and his seed were the promises made. He saith not, and to seeds, as of many; but as of one, and to thy seed, which is Christ.

—Galatians 3:16

The story of Abraham and Israel has immense historic significance for all Christians. Besides Jesus Himself, Judaism gave Christians the one true and living God. It contributed a sacred book, its own testament, and thereby paved the way for the New Testament. It passed on a historical tradition that made life purposeful with a history full of meaning. The Gospels are a record of Jewish life in Judea and in Galilee during the early decades of the first century.

For we have not followed cunningly devised fables, when we made known unto you the power and coming of our Lord Jesus Christ, but were eyewitnesses of his majesty.

—2 Peter 1:16

The early Christians, when they set out to convert the Gentiles, took the Old Testament as their text, which gave them an unequal advantage over their rivals. No other religion in the empire possessed a book charged with such vitality and eloquence. Israel had given to Christianity the prophets of truth and righteousness as well as a belief in the Messiah. This is exactly what the apostle Peter was referring to in our passage when he stated, "...*but [we] were eyewitnesses [to] his majesty.*" All the disciples of Christ had very unique experiences during their conversions. However, nowhere in Christian history is there evidence of a single conversion to Christ that would have a worldwide impact like that of Saul of Tarsus, later called Paul the Apostle. Saul was a leading participant in the persecution that began with the slaying of Stephen.

> *And in those days, when the number of the disciples was multiplied, there arose a murmuring of the Grecians against the Hebrews, because their widows were neglected in the daily ministration. Then the twelve called the multitude of the disciples unto them, and said, It is not reason that we should leave the word of God, and serve tables. Wherefore, brethren, look ye out among you seven men of honest report, full of the Holy Ghost and wisdom, whom we may appoint over this business. But we will give ourselves continually to prayer, and to the ministry of the word. And the saying pleased the whole multitude: and they chose Stephen, a man full of faith and of the Holy Ghost, and Philip, and Prochorus,*

QUITTING IS NOT AN OPTION

*and Nicanor, and Timon, and Parmenas, and Nico-
las a proselyte of Antioch.*

—Acts 6:1–5

*And Stephen, full of faith and power, did great wonders and
miracles among the people.*

—Acts 6:8

*And Saul was consenting unto his death. And at
that time there was a great persecution against the
church which was at Jerusalem; and they were all
scattered abroad throughout the regions of Judaea
and Samaria, except the apostles. And devout men
carried Stephen to his burial, and made great lam-
entation over him. As for Saul, he made havock of
the church, entering into every house, and haling
men and women committed them to prison.*

—Acts 8:1–3

After the stoning of this faithful disciple, the church
at Jerusalem was scattered widely except the apostles.
The spirit of commitment remained, and they were
steadfast.

And as for Paul, God had already determined his
fate and purpose. As he journeyed to Damascus on his
way to arresting even more Christians, God interrupted
his trip with a dazzling display of power and strength,
knocking him off his steed and rendering him blind.

And he trembling and astonished said, Lord, what wilt thou have me to do? And the Lord said unto him, Arise, and go into the city, and it shall be told thee what thou must do.

—Acts 9:6

Meanwhile, some of the members escaped to Damascus and others fled three hundred miles to Antioch, the capital of Syria, of which the great province of Palestine was a part. At Antioch, these few Judeans went into the Jewish synagogue and there gave their testimony for Jesus as the Messiah.

In every synagogue, a place was set apart for Gentile worshippers. Many of these heard the gospel at Antioch and embraced the faith of Christ.

Then tidings of these things came unto the ears of the church which was in Jerusalem: and they sent forth Barnabas, that he should go as far as Antioch. Then departed Barnabas to Tarsus, for to seek Saul: And when he had found him, he brought him unto Antioch. And it came to pass, that a whole year they assembled themselves with the church, and taught much people. And the disciples were called Christians first in Antioch. And in these days came prophets from Jerusalem unto Antioch.

—Acts 11:22, 25–27

As a result of this powerful rendering of prophetic insight and direction—the same of which God is calling for today—coupled with a spirit of love and devotion, a Church grew up wherein Jews and Gentiles worshipped together as equals in privilege. It has been noted when people share common needs, struggles, and enemies, it can have a galvanizing effect. What a staunch testimonial to Judeo-Christian history. One can only imagine what this God-inspired relationship would look like due to the devastating onslaught that was orchestrated by those whose hatred for a reconciled Church ran so deep that it would be perpetuated throughout the Church's history.

We are troubled on every side, yet not distressed; we are perplexed, but not in despair; persecuted, but not forsaken; cast down, but not destroyed.

—2 Corinthians 4:8–9

Consider the first Church almost stillborn; everything was going wrong that could go wrong. These were some perplexing, bewildering times for the disciples, who were a rare breed indeed. As the pains and suspicions of abandonment ran rapidly again, they found their faith being challenged in ways that many Christians of our day could hardly imagine. Yet, they refused to back down; they refused to quit. Based on a decision rendered by the spirit of prophecy, the Church was given permission to expand its missionary efforts to include people of all races and in every land. But as the Church made its trek throughout the Roman provinces, so did the evil adversary who pursued her.

Be sober, be vigilant; because your adversary the devil, as a roaring lion, walketh about, seeking whom he may devour: Whom resist stedfast in the faith, knowing that the same afflictions are accomplished in your brethren that are in the world.

—1 Peter 5:8–9

So, the Church was forced to build her legacy on a trail of blood, sweat, and tears. For many who opposed the Church, it was just a matter of economics and social acceptance. Heathenism was hospitable to new forms and objects of worship. When the people of a province or city desired to promote trade or immigration, they would build temples to the deities that were worshiped in other lands so their citizens would have a place of worship.

Christianity, however, presented a problem to this kind of religious inclusion because it opposed all worship except to its own God. The Christians were, therefore, regarded as unsocial and gloomy, as atheists having no gods and haters of their fellow men. Even when it came down to showing their loyalty to the reigning emperor by offering incense to images of him that were set up in certain places as one would to a god, they were steadfast in their beliefs and were determined to remain loyal to the doctrine that they had embraced. There would be no incense offered to the emperor or any other deity, no, not even a pinch.

And so, through all those acts of wickedness waged against them, God's people were still able to hear a voice of comfort from places their enemies never knew existed, nor could they ever understand how.

Be ye strong therefore, and let not your hands be weak: for your work shall be rewarded.

—2 Chronicles 15:7

As time went on, the leaders of the Church were taken down to break her spirit and weaken her morale. The first of these was James, the brother of Jesus. James was a loyal supporter of Jewish customs and practices and a recognized leader among Jewish Christians. He was slain in the temple around 62 AD. But even in this, a still comforting voice remained constant as it etched its way into the hearts of those who continued to trust.

For God is not unrighteous to forget your work and labour of love, which ye have shewed toward his name, in that ye have ministered to the saints, and do minister.

—Hebrews 6:10

In the year 64 AD, a large part of Rome was destroyed by a great fire. It had been reported that the fire had been started by Nero, the worst of all the Roman emperors. To clear himself, Nero blamed the Christians for the devastation. This promptly gave rise to a terrible persecution; thousands were tortured and put to death. Nero had declared an all-out war on the Christian nation. Multitudes of Christians were burned as "living torches" while the emperor drove his chariot among them nude and playing a fiddle.

In Rome, the capital of the most powerful empire of the western world, in 67 AD, the apostle Peter, a man who was recognized by Paul as one of the pillars of the Church, was crucified upside down. In 68 AD, just one year later, Peter's death would be followed by the beheading of Paul in Rome. Some called it poetic justice, and others called it a twist of faith, but to this observer, it seemed ironic that the gardens of Nero, the courts where the apostle Paul and the apostle Peter were both slain or martyred, the places where countless thousands of Christians were slaughtered like animals, are now the seat of the Vatican palace, the home of the Roman Catholic pontiff, and recognized by millions as the center of the Christian world.

But under this current order, sanctioned and equipped with the word of prophecy, a word that is, in fact, sharper than a two-edged sword, God, by way of

His Spirit, has given license to His elect to stand as tall as anyone else in the world, to act as beacons of light, and to illuminate the way for the greatest event this world has ever known, the second coming of our *Lord Jesus Christ*.

Just as the believers who blazed the trail before us refused to dishonor the directives of God and the patterns set by Jesus Himself, neither should we dishonor or ignore this mandate that God has set before us. We must adopt the same position that they so honorably lived and died for, which stands as a firm commitment of the faithful that when it comes to this end-time, amazing, all-inspiring move of God, *Quitting Is Not an Option*.

CHAPTER 14

Forging Ahead by Faith

Brethren, I count not myself to have apprehended: but this one thing I do, forgetting those things which are behind, and reaching forth unto those things which are before, I press toward the mark for the prize of the high calling of God in Christ Jesus

—Philippians 3:13–14

Here, the apostle Paul is bearing his soul to those who he felt like himself were stanch believers in the doctrine they were imparting to others. Paul, understanding their frailties and unspoken concerns as to whether they could really reach a certain level of acceptance in the eyes of a perfect God, begins his message by calling them brethren. This was to confirm that at the very core of his being, he was one of them. Paul, using himself as an example, had one goal in mind, to inspire them to continue forward in their mission, which was the furtherance of the gospel. Paul's plan was to eliminate any and all possible excuses that might impede the progress of those who were starting to feel unworthy of the task at hand. Paul expresses his sentiments as he conveys to them that no matter how harshly the wind might blow, he would put his shoulder to those opposing forces and press.

> *The LORD is my shepherd; I shall not want. He maketh me to lie down in green pastures: he leadeth me beside the still waters. He restoreth my soul: he leadeth me in the paths of righteousness for his name's sake. Yea, though I walk through the valley of the shadow of death, I will fear no evil: for thou art with me; thy rod and thy staff they comfort me. Thou preparest a table before me in the presence of mine enemies: thou anointest my head with oil; my cup runneth over. Surely goodness and mercy shall follow me all the days of my life: and I will dwell in the house of the LORD for ever.*
>
> —Psalm 23

For centuries, this psalm has held its unrivaled position as one of the premier writings of all religious literature in the world. No matter what age, race, or circumstance one might find themselves identified with, there is something about this psalm that is able to bring inner peace and quiet comfort to the soul. It has been read by and spoken into the ear of many disheartened and frightened seekers of absolution. It is indeed in a class all its own, as it breathes confidence and trust that we are not being asked to take this journey all alone.

"Yea though I walk through the valley of the shadow of death, I will fear no evil: for thou art with me..." It is an undisputed fact that God's people have trudged through this valley and under the shadow of death for an untold number of years.

And from the days of John the Baptist until now the kingdom of heaven suffereth violence and the violent taketh it by force.

—Matthew 11:12

Throughout the ages and often under unmitigating circumstances, God has had a drawn-out people, those that He would use to be a conduit through which to send the Redeemer of the world, all the while being the recipients of His grace on the other end. Sounds like a type of tag-team event, doesn't it? They had not earned or asked for this, but because of the sovereignty and grace of God, He tagged them and, in numerous ways, announced that they would be His people.

For both he that sanctifieth and they who are sanctified are all of one: for which cause he is not ashamed to call them breth-

ren, saying, I will declare thy name unto my brethren, in the midst of the church will I sing praise unto thee.

—Hebrews 2:11–12

When the Israelites went down into the land of Egypt, there were seventy; when they received their freedom, they were a mixed multitude of possibly more than a million. They would then go into the land of Canaan and conquer that land under God's power and authority. This was a strange people that God had created for Himself.

I am as a wonder unto many; but thou art my strong refuge. Let my mouth be filled with thy praise and with thy honour all the day.

—Psalm 71:7–8

In 1 Peter 2:9, God's chosen are called "a peculiar people." And nowhere is this fact more exemplified than in certain parts of the Middle East and most of Africa. Iran, it's been calculated, has one of the fastest-growing underground churches in the world, while in China alone, there are over one million underground Christians, those who every single day are risking life and limb for what they believe.

And in spite of the constant harassments and the dire consequences they face because of their stand for Christ, like the apostle Paul, they continue to press; the

Lord, working with them, confirming the word with signs following.

Also, since the mainstream media has shown no interest in conveying the amazing acts of God and the continuing move of the Spirit taking place in so many of these assemblies, it is incumbent upon us (God's chosen) along with them to forge ahead by faith. Our brethren in the Middle East, as well as in other parts of the world, are entrenched and committed to what they know without a doubt to be true, that there is one crimson cord that unites us all, and that this cord of love can never be broken.

For all the promises of God in him are yea, and in him Amen, unto the glory of God by us. Now he which stablisheth us with you in Christ, and hath anointed us, is God.
—2 Corinthians 1:20–21

It is important to note that this universal church literally draws strength and encouragement from those in the West, like yourselves, and from places like Israel, whom they believe can hear directly from God and bring back to them a rhema word. A word that will lead, guide, and encourage them as they forge their way through the valley of the shadow of death.

It is a true saying that God is extravagant but not wasteful. We can ill afford to squander those precious gifts that were breathed upon us by the Holy Spirit.

Then said Jesus to them again, Peace be unto you... And when he had said this, he breathed on them, and saith unto them, Receive ye the Holy Ghost: Whose soever sins ye remit, they are remitted unto them; and whose soever sins ye retain, they are retained.

—John 20:21–23

What a powerful responsibility that was; God had entrusted them, given to them the kind of divine authority that most men might never experience. There are many of you that have been given tremendous talents from God Himself but are afraid to display those talents for fear of what others might think.

Then answered them the Pharisees, Are ye also deceived? Have any of the rulers or of the Pharisees believed on him? But this people who knoweth not the law are cursed. Nicodemus saith unto them, (he that came to Jesus by night, being one of them,) Doth our law judge any man, before it hear him, and know what he doeth?

—John 7:47–51

Nicodemus had been shown the light by Jesus, but like so many, he didn't have the courage to *lift up his head*. Here is where one's true test of faith will come.

Trust me when I say, prophetically speaking, that some of you are being tested in that same regard right now. My prayer is that you be loosed of that disillusionment and be reintroduced to that magnificent creature that God has set you apart to become.

As David said in Psalm 71, *"Let my mouth be filled with thy praise and with thy honour all the day"* (verse 8). This is not a time to dishonor God by keeping to yourselves that which is so desperately needed among His people as well as those who are currently walking blind.

Let no corrupt communication proceed out of your mouth, but that which is good to the use of edifying, that it may minister grace unto the hearers. And grieve not the holy Spirit of God, whereby ye are sealed unto the day of redemption.
—Ephesians 4:29–30

If God can be expected to keep His end of the bargain, then so should we be expected to do all we can to keep ours as well.

In God will I praise his word: in the LORD will I praise his word. In God have I put my trust: I will not be afraid what man can do unto me.
—Psalm 56:10–11

This is an oath that David took when the Philistines took him in Gath. One that he knew God expected him to keep. How many times have you asked God to act in your behalf, and He did? How sincere were you when you made your oaths to Him?

After all, you are a people whom He would fight for and slay kings for. He would literally open and part rivers and seas and bring down walls for you, His people. And now the battlelines are being drawn, and decisions will have to be made by those bearing gifts from God! It's either fight or flight. That's why I hear God saying, *"If what you have and who you are is not becoming to the world, then it should not be becoming to Me."*

Behold, I am the LORD, the God of all flesh: is there any thing too hard for me?
—Jeremiah 32:27

Through the prophet Jeremiah, we find God making an open declaration that when it comes to Him, nothing falls beyond the realm of possibilities. No matter how great the turbulence might be around those who embrace His presence and accept His divine sovereignty, He always has and always will be a bridge over troubled waters. It is clear in this Scripture that God is directly challenging the spirit of doubt. God's strategy here is to disable the great disabler—fear. I say great because of the number of lives this spirit has claimed and the number of casualties it has produced. It has been said that all evil needs to succeed is for good people, *because of fear*, to do nothing.

And the LORD God called unto Adam, and said unto him, Where art thou? And he said, I heard thy voice in the garden, and I was afraid, because I was naked; and I hid myself.
—Genesis 3:9–10

Adam feared God in that he felt naked and alone. That is what fear does. It separates us not only from God but also, in many cases, from each other. We have all been reared in a world plagued with human suffering and death. We develop fear that is born out of uncertainty and grieve in our hearts because we were never built to handle loss. So, we strive to avoid any circumstance that will create fear in an attempt to control pain.

Sometimes, fear can be a good thing, but oftentimes those things that we shy away or try to hide from are the very things that are needed to bring us to a required or desired place. God is calling us to a collective effort. He is calling us to a corporate move. The one thing we cannot do is to be so afraid that we are not willing to embrace the mission that has been clearly set before us. In other words, the mission must be greater than the misery.

For God hath not given us the spirit of fear; but of power, and of love, and of a sound mind.

—2 Timothy 1:7

Let's listen to these prophetic words that constitute the mind of God.

And there shall come forth a rod out of the stem of Jesse, and a Branch shall grow out of his roots: And the spirit of the LORD shall rest upon him, the spirit of wisdom and understanding, the spirit of counsel and might, the spirit of knowledge and of the fear of the Lord.

—Isaiah 11:1–2

I am the vine, ye are the branches: He that abideth in me, and I in him, the same bringeth forth much fruit: for without me ye can do nothing.

—John 15:5

In his prophecy, Isaiah informs us that from the bloodline of Jesse would come a rod (King David) and from the roots of that rod, a Branch, which was Jesus. Some seven hundred years later, in the New Testament book of John, we are made witnesses to an extraordinary transfer or handoff. All those attributes that the Spirit of God rested upon Jesus, He now gives or sets upon the Church, which would be led by His disciples.

He that abideth in me, and I in him, the same bringeth forth much fruit of itself.

—John 15:5

We are clearly in the season of Isaiah's prophecy, which was revisited by Jesus in John 15. Although many of the events of the prophecy have yet to take place, it is certain that the stage is set, and the curtain is going up, as Isaiah speaks directly to what we have been proposing all along.

The spirit of counsel and might are two terms that cannot be misunderstood. "To counsel" is "to instruct, guide, and direct from a position of knowledge and authority." "Might," through Christ, is "power, influence, rule, and strength."

Behold, I give unto you power to tread on serpents and scorpions, and over all the power of the enemy: and nothing shall by any means hurt you.

—Luke 10:19

These would be the general workings, characteristics, and attributes of God's prophetic assembly.

And shall make him of quick understanding in the fear of the LORD: and he shall not judge after the sight of his eyes, neither reprove after the hearing of his ears.

—Isaiah 11:3

The Scripture goes on to say that the Branch *and those chosen by Him* shall trust in the judgments received from God. "*...understanding in the fear of the Lord...*" and that He (the Branch) shall not be dictated to or influenced by outside forces or circumstances. The inner voices of His Church shall be governed and led by the Holy Spirit of God.

> *And it shall come to pass in that day, that the Lord shall set his hand again the second time to recover the remnant of his people, which shall be left, from Assyria, and from Egypt, and from Pathros, and from Cush, and from Elam, and from Shinar, and from Hamath, and from the islands of the sea.*
>
> —Isaiah 11:11

The first time God set His hand upon Israel was a physical recovery of her back to the Holy Land in 1948; it was then that she was recognized by the world as a sovereign nation. However, the second recovery will be a spiritual one that will be implemented by the Church, which has been identified in Scripture as the branches of the vine or stem of Jesse.

The duties of the prophetic branch or council must include the setting free of captives by the execution of a guided and accurate word from God.

Stand fast therefore in the liberty wherewith Christ hath made us free, and be not entangled again with the yoke of bondage.

—Galatians 5:1

This word will always orchestrate the movement of the Church while admonishing it to forge ahead, always pressing toward the Great Commission and continuing to wage its own holy war against all who seek to defy its *"rites of passage."*

With the blessing of the council and their being led by the Spirit, the Church continued to grow until its area of recruitment included the entire Roman empire. From the Atlantic coast of Spain in the west to the Black Sea in the east. From the Rhine in the north to the Nile in the south.

Paul also and Barnabas continued in Antioch, teaching and preaching the word of the Lord, with many others also. And some days after Paul said unto Barnabas, Let us go again and visit our brethren in every city where we have preached the word of the LORD, and see how they do.

—Acts 15:35–36

The relentless campaign of the Christian Church was made even easier because the Romans had connected these large swatches of land by building a highly developed network of well-constructed roads. Now all of this was done in accordance with a parable that Jesus shared with those in His midst.

> *He said therefore, A certain nobleman went into a far country to receive for himself a kingdom, and to return. And he called his ten servants, and delivered them ten pounds, and said unto them, Occupy till I come.*
> —Luke 19:12–13

"To occupy" is "to have a distinct presence in a certain place." The key to carrying out His instruction is spiritual awareness, keenness, and sensitivity to be able to create an air or atmosphere in the place or arena that you are occupying, which opens us up to this immense prophetic perception that now it becomes our turn to travel along those Roman roads by gaining access to those wild and crazy platforms made available to millions; they were built for one purpose but are now made ripe for the harvest.

> *For by him were all things created, that are in heaven, and that are in earth, visible and invisible, whether they be thrones, or dominions, or principalities, or powers: all things were created by him, and for him: And he is before all things, and by him all things consist.*
> —Colossians 1:16–17

The Scripture tells us that our God was way ahead of all those things, even before they were ever produced. "Consist" details what something is composed or made up of, its ingredients. That means every wire, transistor, transmitter, and circuit was all there with Him in the beginning.

God is our refuge and strength, a very present help in trouble.

—Psalm 46:1

With us being safe and secure in the fellowship of His counsel, we can better hear God as He informs, equips, and enables us. And from that unfailing, flawless information, we gain revealed knowledge, which is our power and strength. The help being sought after is certainly needed for the here and now. And therefore, under the watchful eye of Jehovah-Jireh (our Provider), we can rest assured that all these directives will be accompanied by multiplied blessings, prophecy, and words of wisdom, each tried and tested under the anointing of the Holy Spirit. And that's all the reason why, as the opening of this chapter sternly advocates, *we of this chosen body* solemnly commit ourselves to *Forging Ahead by Faith.*

Conclusion

It is imperative that we understand for the first time in our generation that every prayer set before God has an excellent possibility of being answered. We are definitely living in a season of recovery, and our embracing this prophetic clarion call from God is a huge part of that process. As the Bible warns us in 1 Timothy 4:1, during this latter time, many shall depart from the faith in their futile efforts to be moved from the mundane to the mystical. But our God is not the author of confusion, and only His uninhibited, emboldened, vividly inspired word of prophecy can challenge that trend. For He is a God who prefers an atmosphere of worship; that's why He dwells in the midst of His people and their praises.

For as the body without the spirit is dead, so faith without works is dead also.

—James 2:26

With that being said, I ask that you join me as we go before our Father in prayer, trusting fully that He will hear our petitions and strengthen our hearts.

All wise and eternal God, our Father, we come to You in the only way we know how, and that is in the mighty name of Jesus, He who was, is, and is to come. As always, Father, we want to begin our humble plea by thanking You for every gracious benefit You've shown us because, as Jesus has said, without them, we can do nothing.

That's why we are seeking divine favor, that through Your loving-kindness, You might lay Your tender mercies upon us as well as all those that are dear to our hearts. Lord, as we step out on this thing that You have called us to, we ask that You send Your angel to trouble the waters, that Your presence be made known and felt by those You've chosen for this hour. We ask also that You give them clear discernment of those dreams and visions that You have imparted to them, that they might bloom as roses in the desert. And most of all, we pray that You will give them the courage to lift up their heads and blow their trumpets until the King of Glory and Captain of the battlefield makes His glorious entrance.

All these things we do ask in the mighty name of Jesus, our Lord! Amen.

Bibliography

Goll, James W. *Coming Israel Awakening, The Gazing into the Future of the Jewish People and the Church*. Grand Rapids: Chosen Books, 2009.

Harpur, James, and Marcus Braybrooke. *The Collegeville Atlas of the Bible*. Collegeville: Liturgical Press, 1999.

Roth, Sid. *The Race to Save The World: CHRISTIANS AND JEWS MUST UNITE TO FORM THE ONE NEW MAN*. New York: Charisma House, 2004.

Biography

Bishop Royce L. Woods was born in Raleigh, North Carolina, and is the seventeenth of eighteen children born to the late Bishop John and Mary Woods. At an early age, his family moved from Raleigh to Washington, DC.

After serving four years in the United States Navy, he received both the Vietnam Campaign and Service Medals and an Honorable Discharge.

Bishop Woods began his ministry on the streets of the nation's capital. His work has taken him across the country, where he has forged strong relationships with both Jew and Gentile Christians. The last thirty-plus years have been spent building community-based training and outreach programs through the development of the Chosen Generation, which provides and creates hands-on opportunities for concerned business and government officials to make a difference in their communities.

He holds a bachelor's degree in biblical studies, a master of divinity, a master of Christian psychology and pastoral counseling, and a doctorate of theology.

Dr. Woods is the senior pastor of Holy Trinity Worship Center International, located at 4628 Minnesota Avenue, NE, Washington, DC, 20019. Offices 202-398-2739/240-348-4746.

He lives in Prince George's County, Maryland, with his wife, Catherine.

Bishop Woods is, without a doubt, a man on a mission for Christ. He gains strength from his most quoted scripture, Romans 8:31 (KJV): *"What shall we say to these things? If God be for us, who can be against us?"*

CPSIA information can be obtained
at www.ICGtesting.com
Printed in the USA
LVHW082041060522
718035LV00012B/295